outdoor food

OVER 80 MOUTHWATERING RECIPES
FOR PARTIES AND BARBECUES

LINDA DOESER

This is a Parragon Book
This edition published in 2005

Parragon
Queen Street House
4 Queen Street
Bath BA1 1HE, UK

Copyright © Parragon 2004

Created and produced for Parragon by The Bridgewater Book Company Ltd.
Cover by Talking Design

ISBN: 1-40545-081-9

Printed in China

NOTE

*This book uses metric and imperial measurements. Follow the same units of
measurement throughout; do not mix metric and imperial. All spoon measurements
are level: teaspoons are assumed to be 5 ml and tablespoons are assumed to be 15 ml.
Unless otherwise stated, milk is assumed to be full fat, eggs and individual vegetables
such as potatoes are medium, and pepper is freshly ground black pepper.*

*The times given for each recipe are an approximate guide only. The preparation times
may differ according to the techniques used by different people and the cooking times may vary
as a result of the type of oven used. Ovens should be preheated to the specified temperature.
If using a fan-assisted oven, check the manufacturer's instructions for adjusting the time and
temperature. The preparation times include chilling and marinating times, where appropriate.*

*Recipes using raw or very lightly cooked eggs should be avoided by infants, the elderly,
pregnant women, convalescents and anyone suffering from an illness. Pregnant and breastfeeding
women are advised to avoid eating peanuts and peanut products.*

Contents

Introduction

Sharing food with family and friends has always been one of the greatest pleasures of life and, when combined with all the fun of eating in the open air, it becomes twice as enjoyable. There are lots of ways to enjoy alfresco food, such as at a simple gathering of friends in the garden on a summer evening, an afternoon picnic by the river or an informal portable barbecue brunch on the beach. More substantial

serve cold food or hot snacks or to cook on the barbecue, most of the work will be completed before your guests arrive, giving you time to catch up with each other's news – and to check that everyone is supplied with a drink.

This book is divided into two main sections. The first offers practical, general advice on entertaining, with three chapters of great recipes for hot and cold

parties are great, too. You don't have to wear yourself out in advance either; whether you are planning an elegant evening buffet or a full-scale, three-course barbecue for twenty.

Careful planning is the secret of success and this book is packed with fabulous recipes and clever ideas for just such occasions. Whether you intend to

snacks, dips, nibbles and buffets. The second section concentrates on outdoor cooking, with useful tips about the best equipment and ensuring safety, with four chapters full of sizzling barbecue recipes, plus some marvellous salad accompaniments.

Of course, you don't have to confine yourself to just one type of party. Mix and match recipes from different chapters to suit the occasion. For example, you could occupy your guests with a selection of scrumptious dips from the first part of the book, while you get on with grilling one of the delicious marinated dishes from the second. Similarly, all the salads can just as easily be packed into rigid plastic containers for a picnic as they can be served in bowls at a barbecue. They would be a good addition to a buffet table, too.

When entertaining outdoors, the one thing you can't do very far in advance is to take out the food. Not only is it a health risk to leave dishes in hot

sunshine or exposed to flies and other insects, neighbourhood cats seem to have an in-built radar for any parties in the vicinity. Once you have taken the food out, put a helpful friend on guard duty. You may, of course, prefer to lay a buffet table indoors with easy access to the garden, but barbecues should be exclusively alfresco. Make copious use of clingfilm, cool boxes and trays of crushed ice. Cool boxes, plastic containers and screw-top jars for dressings and marinades are essential for picnics and portable barbecues.

Outdoor entertaining is the perfect solution when you have lots of friends with children. For a start, it prevents small feet from treading sausage rolls or chicken drumsticks into your carpets. The occasion tends to be more informal, so the kids are more likely to enjoy themselves, with the result that their parents will too. If you have the space, why not provide a play corner for very young children with a sand tray? If you can be sure someone will be willing to supervise, you could even fill a paddling pool. As far as food is concerned, there are lots of recipes in this book that will appeal to children, from little snacks on skewers to tender home-made burgers.

Mixing and matching recipes is a good idea if you are entertaining both vegetarians and meat-eaters, although each part of the book contains a wide choice of recipes to suit both. In fact, there is something to suit all ages and tastes, from hot and spicy to rich and creamy and from elegant and sophisticated to fresh and fun.

Party Food

Whether it is a long-planned outdoor celebration or an impromptu gathering, a party is always a uniquely special occasion. For the host, however, a party may also be a time of stress and hard work. With you having to spend time ensuring that everyone is mingling, and that the conversation is flowing as freely as the drink, the last thing you need is to be worrying about the food that you are

serving. It should be as much fun for you to throw a party as it is to attend one. Only you can decide whether your guests will get on with each other or if you can afford to serve champagne, but the first section of this book can at least take away any worries about what snacks to serve to keep your guests happy.

The following section is divided into three chapters, all of which feature a selection of vegetarian as well as fish and meat recipes. So, no matter what the tastes of your guests, you can be sure to find dishes here to please everyone. Most of the recipes are for finger foods – easy to eat outdoors and will minimize the amount of preparation and clearing up afterwards. As well as these, there are a few

dishes that simply require a fork to eat them. The emphasis throughout is on treats that are easy to prepare and serve outdoors. After all, you want your guests to enjoy the food but don't want to spend so much time in the kitchen that you are too tired to enjoy yourself.

The chapter on Dips & Pâtés offers a fabulous collection of recipes from around the world which are perfect for easy outdoor entertaining. Delicious treats range from Middle Eastern Baba Ghanoush (see page 26) to Traditional English Potted Shrimps (see page 36). All of these dishes are made in advance and can be laid out in a tempting array with a selection of different breads. Individual recipes provide specific serving suggestions, or you can try some of the party basics on pages 10–11.

Cold Nibbles is the chapter to turn to for the main constituents of your buffet table. This chapter provides a wide choice of recipes for savoury pastries

and biscuits; stuffed and pickled vegetables; and tarts and nibbles. There are recipes for traditional favourites, such as Cheese Straws (see page 48) and Sausage Rolls (see page 72). For those with more exotic tastes, there is a selection of exciting and more unusual delicacies to choose from. These range from the spicy delight of Deep-fried Prawn Balls (see page 64) to the sunny flavour of Stuffed Vine Leaves (see page 68). While all of these snacks are delicious cold, some can also be served warm or hot if you prefer.

The final chapter in this section features a selection of Hot Nibbles. These are always a special treat, but it is easy to be over-ambitious, so the dishes are nice and simple. Many of the recipes can be prepared during the party. Others can be prepared in advance, and then popped in the oven or grilled after your guests have arrived.

Whatever kind of outdoor party you are planning, from a small family gathering to a grand seasonal celebration, you will find the best bites and most moreish morsels for the occasion in this section. You can use the recipes to plan exactly what canapés and snacks will make the best combination for each event. Prepare everything well in advance, and you will be free to enjoy the party as much as your guests.

Party Basics

Hosting a party, and making some tempting nibbles for your guests, should be fun. All you need is a selection of recipes, and some careful preparation. Don't forget that there are plenty of delicious ready-made nibbles that you can buy to increase the variety of your party snacks and lessen the time you will need to spend preparing the party food. Plain and flavoured breadsticks, corn and tortilla chips, as well as plain potato crisps, are great for dunking into home-made dips or just for nibbling on their own. Peanuts are party favourites, but you can also include cashew nuts, almonds and pistachios. A selection of cheeses and a basket of crackers or crusty bread, served with a dish of butter, is easy and always popular.

If you are already planning to prepare a range of flavoursome foods, you can supplement them with some simpler snacks, such as grilled chicken drumsticks, sausages on sticks, and squares of toast with ready-made toppings such as lumpfish roe (red caviar), sliced hard-boiled eggs, smoked salmon, slices of salami and soft cheese and chives. Garnish with herb sprigs, sliced stuffed olives, pearl onions or tiny gherkins. Sandwiches, however, are best avoided as they quickly dry out.

If you don't mind providing cutlery as well as plates, you can also serve a selection of imaginative salads. Most supermarkets sell a wide selection of mixed leaf and vegetable salads that are ideal for serving at a party. Pasta and rice salads with a colourful mixture of drained canned sweetcorn kernels, red and yellow pepper strips, tomato wedges, cooked frozen peas and strips of cooked ham are easily made and can be dressed with vinaigrette or mayonnaise.

Crudités

Raw and blanched vegetables are perfect for serving with most dips and look very tempting on a large serving platter. Deseed and slice red, yellow or orange peppers lengthways. Baby corn cobs and trimmed, thin asparagus should be blanched in lightly salted boiling water. Include whole cherry tomatoes, small button mushrooms and trimmed radishes, perhaps with a few small leaves attached. Trim and separate the leaves of red and white chicory or the hearts of Little Gem lettuces. Cut raw cauliflower into small florets and slice carrots, celery and cucumber into sticks.

Vegetable Crisps

Home-made vegetable crisps make a delicious alternative to ordinary crisps. You can, of course, use potatoes, but you might also like to try parsnips, carrots or sweet potatoes. Peel the vegetables and slice very thinly using a mandoline or swivel-blade vegetable peeler. Heat sunflower or groundnut oil in a deep-fryer or large saucepan to 180–190°C/ 350–375°F, or until a cube of day-old bread browns in 30 seconds. Add the vegetable slices to the oil and fry until golden. Drain on kitchen paper and sprinkle with sea salt, paprika or cayenne pepper. Store in an airtight container when cold.

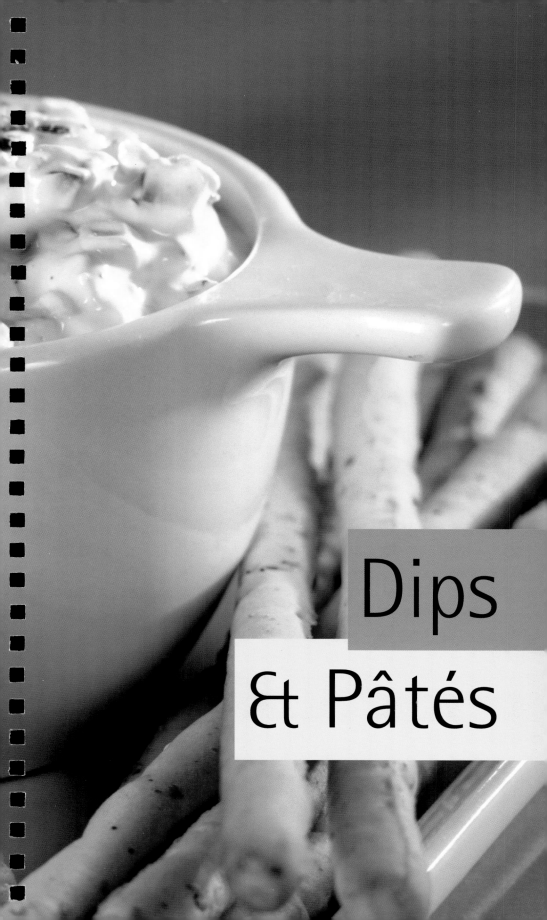

Dips
& Pâtés

Aïoli

This garlic mayonnaise from the Provence region of France is perfectly partnered with a selection of raw vegetables. It is reputed to keep flies away, so makes the ideal choice for a summer buffet table.

serves 8

4 garlic cloves

salt

2 egg yolks

225 ml/8 fl oz olive oil

lemon juice

pepper

To serve

crudités (see page 11)

8 hard-boiled eggs, shelled

Method

❶ Place the garlic cloves and a pinch of salt in a glass bowl and crush with the back of a spoon. Add the egg yolks and beat briefly with an electric mixer until creamy.

❷ Add the oil, a few drops at a time, beating constantly with an electric mixer, until the mixture begins to thicken. Then add the remaining oil in a thin continuous stream, beating constantly.

❸ Stir in a little lemon juice to give the mayonnaise a dipping consistency. Season to taste with a little more salt, if necessary, and pepper. Cover with clingfilm and store in the refrigerator until required.

❹ Before serving, return the aïoli to room temperature and transfer to a serving bowl. Arrange the crudités on a large serving platter, arrange the eggs on top and serve with the aïoli.

Tzatziki

This creamy Greek dip is very quick and easy to make, and is wonderfully refreshing on a hot summer's evening.

serves 8

1 cucumber

2 garlic cloves

8 spring onions

600 ml/1 pint natural Greek yogurt

5 tbsp chopped fresh mint,

plus extra to garnish

salt and pepper

To serve

toasted mini pitta breads

sesame breadsticks

Method

❶ Trim the cucumber, but do not peel. Cut it into small, neat dice. Finely chop the garlic and spring onions.

❷ Beat the yogurt in a bowl with a fork until smooth, then fold in the cucumber, garlic, spring onions and mint. Season to taste with salt and pepper.

❸ Transfer to a serving bowl, cover with clingfilm and chill in the refrigerator until required. Garnish with fresh mint and serve with toasted mini pitta breads and sesame breadsticks.

Taramasalata

Home-made taramasalata is infinitely tastier than anything you can buy at a delicatessen, so it is well worth the extra effort. It is traditionally made with grey mullet roe, but cod's roe is easier to find and just as good.

serves 8

225 g/8 oz stale white bread, crusts removed

350 g/12 oz smoked cod's roe

2 garlic cloves, chopped

2 slices onion

4 tbsp lemon juice

175 ml/6 fl oz olive oil

black Kalamata olives, to garnish

chunks of crusty bread, to serve

Method

❶ Roughly tear up the bread and place it in a bowl. Add cold water to cover and leave to soak for 10 minutes.

❷ Meanwhile, using a sharp knife, scrape the roe away from the thick, outer skin. Place the roe in a food processor with the garlic, onion and lemon juice. Drain the bread, squeeze out the excess water with your hands and add it to the food processor. Process the mixture for 2 minutes, or until smooth.

❸ With the motor running, gradually add the oil through the feeder tube until the mixture is smooth and creamy. Scrape into a serving dish, cover with clingfilm and chill in the refrigerator until required.

❹ Garnish the taramasalata with the olives. Serve with chunks of crusty bread.

Guacamole

It is fortunate that this spicy Mexican dip is so quick to prepare because you need to serve it fresh. Otherwise, the avocados will discolour.

serves 8

4 avocados	5 tbsp olive oil
2 garlic cloves	juice of 1½ limes
4 spring onions	salt
3 fresh red chillies, deseeded	chopped fresh coriander leaves, to garnish
2 red peppers, deseeded	tortilla chips, to serve

Method

❶ Cut the avocados in half lengthways and twist the halves to separate. Remove and discard the stones and scoop the flesh into a large bowl with a spoon. Mash coarsely with a fork.

❷ Finely chop the garlic, spring onions, chillies and peppers, then stir them into the mashed avocado. Add 4 tablespoons of the oil and the lime juice, season to taste with salt and stir well to mix. If you prefer a smoother dip, process all the ingredients together in a food processor.

❸ Transfer the guacamole to a serving bowl. Drizzle the remaining oil over the top, sprinkle with the coriander and serve with tortilla chips.

Red Pepper Dip

Serving this pretty pale-pink dip on a platter of red and white vegetables makes it look especially appealing – but beware of the spicy kick.

serves 8

3 red peppers, halved and deseeded

225 g/8 oz fromage frais or curd cheese

½ tsp cayenne pepper

salt

To serve

cherry tomatoes

radishes

radicchio leaves

button mushrooms, halved

cauliflower florets

celery sticks

Method

❶ Preheat the grill. Arrange the pepper halves, skin-side up, on a baking sheet and place under the hot grill for 10–15 minutes, until the skins begin to blacken and blister. Transfer to a polythene bag with tongs, tie the top and leave until the peppers are cool enough to handle.

❷ Remove the peppers from the bag and peel away the skins. Roughly chop the flesh and place in a food processor. Process to a smooth purée, then scrape into a serving bowl.

❸ Stir in the fromage frais or curd cheese until smooth, then stir in the cayenne and salt to taste. Cover with clingfilm and chill in the refrigerator until required.

❹ To serve, place the bowl in the centre of a large platter and arrange the tomatoes, radishes, radicchio, mushrooms, cauliflower and celery around it.

Hummus with Lebanese Seed Bread

Using canned chickpeas in this popular Middle Eastern dip saves time and effort when you are getting party food ready, but you could use dried chickpeas, soaked overnight and cooked in boiling water for about 2½ hours, or until tender.

serves 8

350 g/12 oz canned chickpeas,
drained and rinsed

225 ml/8 fl oz tahini

4 garlic cloves

juice of 3 lemons

6 tbsp water

salt and pepper

2 tbsp olive oil

Lebanese seed bread

70 g/2½ oz toasted sesame seeds

70 g/2½ oz poppy seeds

4 tbsp chopped fresh thyme

150 ml/5 fl oz olive oil

6 pitta breads

To serve

2 tbsp chopped fresh flat-leaved parsley

cayenne pepper

black olives

Method

❶ Preheat the grill to medium. For the bread, place the seeds and thyme in a mortar and crush with a pestle. Stir in the oil. Split open the pitta breads and brush the seed mixture over the cut sides. Cook under the hot grill until golden brown and crisp. Leave to cool. Store in an airtight container until required.

❷ For the hummus, place the chickpeas, tahini, garlic, lemon juice and 4 tablespoons of the water in a food processor. Process until smooth, adding

the remaining water if necessary. Alternatively, mash in a bowl with a fork.

❸ Spoon the mixture into a serving dish and season to taste with salt and pepper. Make a shallow hollow in the top of the hummus and spoon in the oil. If you are not serving it immediately, cover with clingfilm and chill in the refrigerator.

❹ Sprinkle the hummus with the parsley, dust lightly with cayenne and serve with black olives and the Lebanese seed bread.

Baba Ghanoush

**This tasty aubergine dip is not so well known in the West as hummus
(see page 24), but is very popular in the Middle East.**

serves 8

3 large aubergines

3 garlic cloves, chopped

6 tbsp tahini

6 tbsp lemon juice

1 tsp ground cumin

3 tbsp chopped fresh flat-leaved parsley

salt and pepper

fresh flat-leaved parsley sprigs, to garnish

vegetable crisps (see page 11), to serve

Method

❶ Preheat the grill to low. Prick the aubergines all over with a fork and cut in half lengthways. Arrange the halves, skin side up, on a baking sheet and place under the grill for 15 minutes, or until the skins begin to blacken and blister and the flesh feels soft. Remove from the grill and leave until cool enough to handle.

❷ Peel the aubergines and squeeze out any excess moisture, then roughly chop the flesh and place in a food processor. Add the garlic and 2 tablespoons of the tahini and process to mix, then add 2 tablespoons of the lemon juice and process again. Continue adding the tahini and lemon juice alternately, processing between each addition.

❸ When the mixture is smooth, scrape it into a bowl and stir in the cumin and chopped parsley. Season to taste with salt and pepper.

❹ Transfer the dip to a serving dish. If you are not serving it immediately, cover with clingfilm and chill in the refrigerator until required. Return the dip to room temperature to serve. Garnish with parsley sprigs and serve with vegetable crisps.

Quick Chicken Liver Pâté with Melba Toast

Although this is a speedy recipe, you need to leave time for the pâté to cool. If you like, make it up to three days in advance of your party and chill, covered, in the refrigerator.

serves 8

2 tbsp olive oil

2 onions, chopped

2 garlic cloves, finely chopped

675 g/1 lb 8 oz chicken livers

3 tbsp brandy

2 tbsp chopped fresh parsley

1 tbsp chopped fresh sage

salt and pepper

300 g/10½ oz cream cheese

fresh parsley sprigs, to garnish

Melba toast

8 slices medium-thick white bread

Method

❶ Heat the oil in a large, heavy-based frying pan over a low heat. Add the onions and garlic and cook, stirring occasionally, for 5 minutes, until softened.

❷ Add the livers and cook, stirring and turning occasionally, for 5 minutes, or until lightly browned. Remove the frying pan from the heat, stir in the brandy, parsley and sage and season to taste with salt and pepper. Leave to cool slightly.

❸ Transfer the mixture to a food processor and process until smooth, scraping down the sides of the bowl once or twice. Scrape the mixture into a bowl, cover with clingfilm and leave to cool completely.

❹ Meanwhile, for the Melba Toast, preheat the grill to medium. Lightly toast the bread on both sides under the hot grill. Cut off and discard the crusts, then slice each half to make two very thin slices, each with one untoasted side. Toast the uncooked sides of the bread until the edges begin to curl slightly. Remove from the grill and leave to cool. When completely cool, store in an airtight container until required.

❺ When the chicken liver mixture is cold, stir in the cream cheese and mix well. Cover with clingfilm and chill in the refrigerator until required. Return to room temperature to serve. Garnish with parsley sprigs and serve with the Melba Toast.

Smoked Fish Pâté

Kippers are used here because they have such a rich flavour, provided that they have been hot smoked in the traditional way. You could also use buckling or smoked mackerel, in which case omit the preliminary cooking in Step 1.

serves 8

900 g/2 lb undyed kipper fillets

2 garlic cloves, finely chopped

175 ml/6 fl oz olive oil

6 tbsp single cream

salt and pepper

lemon slices, to garnish

oatcakes, to serve

Method

❶ Place the kippers in a large frying pan or fish kettle and add cold water to just cover. Bring to the boil, then immediately reduce the heat and poach gently for 10 minutes, until tender. If using a frying pan, you may need to do this in batches.

❷ Transfer the fish to a chopping board using a fish slice. Remove and discard the skin. Roughly flake the flesh with a fork and remove any remaining tiny bones. Transfer the fish to a saucepan and add the garlic. Place over a low heat and break up the fish with a wooden spoon.

❸ Gradually add the oil, beating well after each addition. Add the cream and beat until smooth, but do not allow the mixture to boil.

❹ Remove the saucepan from the heat and season to taste with salt, if necessary, and pepper. Spoon the pâté into a serving dish, cover and leave to cool completely. Chill in the refrigerator until required (it can be refrigerated for up to 3 days).

❺ Garnish with lemon slices and serve with oatcakes.

Mushroom &
Chestnut Pâté

This is a gloriously luxurious vegetarian party treat. Dried porcini are quite expensive, but they have a wonderfully intense flavour and you don't need many.

serves 8

225 g/8 oz dried chestnuts,
soaked overnight

25 g/1 oz dried porcini mushrooms

4 tbsp hot water

4 tbsp Marsala or medium sherry

1 tbsp olive oil

675 g/1 lb 8 oz chestnut mushrooms,
sliced

1 tbsp balsamic vinegar

1 tbsp chopped fresh parsley

1 tbsp soy sauce

salt and pepper

thinly sliced radish, to garnish

wholemeal toast triangles or
crusty bread, to serve

Method

❶ Drain the chestnuts, place them in a saucepan and add cold water to cover. Bring to the boil, then reduce the heat, cover and simmer for 45 minutes. Drain.

❷ Meanwhile, place the porcini in a small bowl with the hot water and 1 tablespoon of the Marsala. Leave to soak for 20 minutes. Drain well, reserving the soaking liquid. Pat the mushrooms dry with kitchen paper. Strain the soaking liquid through a fine sieve or coffee filter paper.

❸ Heat the oil in a large, heavy-based frying pan. Add the chestnut mushrooms and cook over a low heat, stirring occasionally, for 5 minutes, until softened.

❹ Add the porcini, the soaking liquid and vinegar. Cook, stirring constantly, for 1 minute. Increase the heat and stir in the remaining Marsala. Cook, stirring frequently, for 3 minutes. Remove from the heat.

❺ Transfer the chestnuts to a food processor and process to a purée. Add the mushroom mixture and parsley and process to a smooth paste. Add the soy sauce and salt and pepper to taste and briefly process again to mix.

❻ Scrape the pâté into a serving bowl, cover and chill in the refrigerator. Garnish with radish slices before serving and serve with toast triangles or crusty bread.

Cheese & Bean Pâté

This creamy pâté is based on classic Italian ingredients – ricotta and borlotti or cannellini beans, flavoured with garlic, lemon juice and flat-leaved parsley.

serves 8

800 g/1 lb 12 oz canned borlotti or
cannellini beans, drained and rinsed
350 g/12 oz ricotta cheese
2 garlic cloves, roughly chopped
4 tbsp lemon juice
115 g/4 oz butter, melted
3 tbsp chopped fresh flat-leaved parsley
salt and pepper
sunflower oil, for oiling
cheese-flavoured focaccia fingers, to serve

To garnish
fresh flat-leaved parsley sprigs
lemon wedges

Method

❶ Place the beans, ricotta, garlic, lemon juice and melted butter in a food processor and process to a smooth purée. Add the chopped parsley and salt and pepper to taste and process again briefly to mix.

❷ Lightly oil a plain ring mould. Scrape the mixture into the mould and smooth the surface. Cover with clingfilm and chill in the refrigerator until set.

❸ To serve, turn out the pâté on to a serving dish and fill the centre with parsley sprigs. Garnish with lemon wedges and serve with focaccia fingers.

Traditional English Potted Shrimps

For authenticity, potted shrimps should be served with brown bread spread with unsalted butter, but you could also serve them with wholemeal toast, Melba Toast (see page 28) or even chunks of soda bread.

serves 8

280 g/10 oz unsalted butter
3 pieces of blade mace
pinch of freshly grated nutmeg
pinch of cayenne pepper
450 g/1 lb cooked peeled shrimps
slices of brown bread, spread with
unsalted butter, to serve

To garnish
fresh parsley sprigs
lemon slices

Method

❶ Place 175 g/6 oz of the butter in a small, heavy-based saucepan and add the mace, nutmeg and cayenne. Melt over the lowest possible heat, stirring occasionally.

❷ Add the shrimps and cook, stirring constantly, for 2 minutes, or until heated through. Do not allow the mixture to boil.

❸ Remove the saucepan from the heat, then remove and discard the mace. Spoon the mixture into a serving dish and level the surface. Cover and leave to cool, then chill in the refrigerator until set. (If you wish to serve the shrimps in the traditional way, divide the mixture equally between 8 small ramekin dishes.)

❹ When the potted shrimps have set, place the remaining butter in a small, heavy-based saucepan. Melt over a low heat, then skim off the scum that has formed on the surface. Carefully pour off the clear liquid into a bowl, leaving the white milk solids in the base of the saucepan. Spoon the clarified butter over the top of the potted shrimps to make a thin, covering layer. Cover and return to the refrigerator until set.

❺ Garnish the potted shrimps with parsley sprigs and lemon slices and serve with the buttered slices of bread.

Cold
Nibbles

Three-flavour Pinwheels

These tasty little morsels look so appetizing that your guests are sure to snap them up.

makes 50–60

Ham & cream cheese pinwheels
175 g/6 oz cream cheese
4 large slices lean ham
4 tbsp snipped fresh chives

Beef & horseradish pinwheels
125 ml/4 fl oz double cream
2 tbsp creamed horseradish
4 large slices medium-rare roast beef

Salmon & dill cream pinwheels
225 ml/8 fl oz double cream
2 tbsp chopped fresh dill
pepper
4 large or 8 medium slices smoked salmon
4 tbsp lemon juice

Method

❶ For the Ham & Cream Cheese Pinwheels, spread the cream cheese evenly over the slices of ham. Sprinkle with the chives. Roll up each slice tightly and wrap individually in clingfilm. Leave to chill in the refrigerator for 1 hour.

❷ For the Beef & Horseradish Pinwheels, whip the cream in a bowl until stiff, then fold in the creamed horseradish. Spread the mixture evenly over the slices of beef. Roll up each slice tightly and wrap individually in clingfilm. Leave to chill in the refrigerator for 1 hour.

❸ For the Smoked Salmon & Dill Cream Pinwheels, whip the cream in a bowl until stiff, then fold in the dill and pepper to taste. Spread the mixture evenly over the slices of smoked salmon. Roll up each slice tightly and wrap individually in clingfilm. Chill in the refrigerator for 1 hour.

❹ When ready to serve, unwrap the rolls one at a time and thinly slice. Before slicing the Smoked Salmon & Dill Cream Pinwheels, sprinkle with a little lemon juice. Spear each pinwheel on a cocktail stick and arrange on a serving platter.

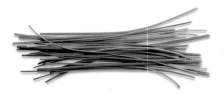

Egg & Tapenade Toasties

Tapenade is a black olive, caper and anchovy paste from Provence. It goes especially well with hard-boiled eggs, but you could also top these toasties with flaked tuna.

makes 8

1 small French loaf

4 tomatoes, thinly sliced

4 eggs, hard-boiled

4 bottled or canned anchovy fillets in olive oil, drained and halved lengthways

8 marinated stoned black olives

Tapenade

100 g/3½ oz stoned black olives

6 bottled or canned anchovy fillets in olive oil, drained

2 tbsp capers, rinsed

2 garlic cloves, roughly chopped

1 tsp Dijon mustard

2 tbsp lemon juice

1 tsp fresh thyme leaves

pepper

4–5 tbsp olive oil

Method

❶ For the Tapenade, place the olives, anchovies, capers, garlic, mustard, lemon juice, thyme and pepper to taste in a food processor and process for 20–25 seconds, or until smooth. Scrape down the sides of the mixing bowl, then with the motor running, gradually add the oil through the feeder tube to make a smooth paste. Spoon the paste into a bowl, cover with clingfilm and reserve until required.

❷ Preheat the grill to medium. Cut the French loaf into 8 slices, discarding the crusty ends. Toast on both sides under the hot grill until golden brown. Leave to cool.

❸ To assemble the toasties, spread a little of the tapenade on one side of each slice of toast. Top with the tomato slices. Shell the eggs, then slice and arrange over the tomatoes. Dot a little of the remaining tapenade on each egg slice. Wind the anchovy fillets on top of the egg slices in an 'S' shape. Halve the marinated olives, arrange 2 halves on each toasty, and serve.

Filled Croustades

These crisp containers are more fun than sandwiches and go well with an endless variety of easy-to-make fillings. In addition to those below, scrambled eggs topped with slivers of ham or salami and cucumber; Smoked Fish Pâté (see page 30), garnished with sliced stuffed olives; or Guacamole (see page 20), topped with chopped tomato and pickled jalapeño chillies, would work well.

makes 48

Croustades
600 g/1 lb 5 oz butter
12 large slices white bread

Cheese & tomato filling
Tapenade (see page 42)
mozzarella cheese, thinly sliced
cherry tomatoes, halved
fresh basil leaves, to garnish

Crab salad filling
115 g/4 oz crabmeat, drained if canned
and thawed if frozen
125 ml/4 fl oz mayonnaise
pinch of celery salt
2 eggs, hard-boiled
fresh dill sprigs, to garnish

Method

❶ Preheat the oven to 180°C/350°F/Gas Mark 4. Make the Croustades in four batches. Melt one-quarter of the butter in a heavy-based saucepan over a low heat. Meanwhile, stamp out 12 rounds of bread with a 7.5-cm/3-inch fluted pastry cutter. When the butter has melted, remove the saucepan from the heat. Dip the bread rounds into the melted butter and press them firmly into the cups of a bun tin.

❷ Place a second bun tin on top to keep the bread rounds in shape. Bake in the preheated oven for 15–20 minutes, or until the Croustades are crisp and firm.

Transfer to a wire rack to cool completely while you cook the remaining batches. When the croustades are cold, fill with your chosen filling and serve.

❸ For the Cheese & Tomato Filling, spoon Tapenade into the Croustades, top each one with a slice of mozzarella and a tomato half and garnish with a basil leaf.

❹ For the Crab Salad Filling, place the crabmeat in a bowl and flake with a fork. Stir in the mayonnaise and celery salt. Shell the eggs, finely chop and stir into the filling mixture. Spoon into the Croustades and garnish with dill sprigs.

Easy Nibbles

Lots of different flavours and textures, and food that is easy to handle and eat, are the keys to party success. This duo of tasty treats satisfies all those criteria.

makes 40

Celery & chicory boats	Devilled eggs
450 g/1 lb cream cheese	6 hard-boiled eggs, shelled
4 spring onions, finely chopped	2 spring onions, finely chopped
4 tbsp chopped sun-dried tomatoes in oil	6 walnut halves, finely chopped
3 tbsp chopped fresh parsley	2 fresh green chillies, deseeded and
1 tbsp snipped fresh chives	finely chopped
175 g/6 oz pimiento-stuffed olives,	1 tbsp mayonnaise
chopped	1 tbsp Dijon mustard
1 tbsp Tabasco sauce	1 tsp white wine vinegar
2 heads chicory, separated into leaves	cayenne pepper
12 celery sticks	salt and pepper
fine strips of red pepper, to garnish	thinly sliced baby gherkins, to garnish

Method

❶ For the Celery & Chicory Boats, beat the cream cheese in a bowl with a wooden spoon until smooth. Stir in the spring onions, sun-dried tomatoes, parsley, chives, olives and Tabasco and mix well. Spoon the mixture into the hollows of the chicory leaves and celery sticks and arrange on a serving plate. Garnish with the strips of red pepper.

❷ For the Devilled Eggs, cut the eggs in half lengthways and scoop out the yolks into a bowl without piercing the whites. Mash the yolks well with a fork, then mix in the spring onions, walnuts, chillies, mayonnaise, mustard and vinegar. Season to taste with cayenne, salt and pepper. Spoon the mixture into the egg white halves and garnish with gherkin slices.

Cheese Straws

Nothing could be simpler or more popular than freshly made cheese straws. You can make the dough in advance, bake one batch and store the remainder, wrapped in foil in the refrigerator, to bake during the party and replenish supplies.

makes 60

225 g/8 oz plain flour, plus extra
for dusting

salt and pepper

cayenne pepper

mustard powder

115 g/4 oz butter, diced, plus extra
for greasing

85 g/3 oz Parmesan or pecorino cheese,
grated

2 egg yolks

1–2 tbsp cold water (optional)

1 egg white, lightly beaten, to glaze

Method

❶ Preheat the oven to 220°C/425°F/Gas Mark 7. Sift the flour into a bowl with a pinch each of salt, pepper, cayenne and mustard powder. Add the butter and rub it in with your fingertips until the mixture resembles breadcrumbs. Stir in the cheese. Add the egg yolks and mix well, adding a little of the cold water, as required, to bind. Shape the dough into a ball.

❷ Roll out the dough on a lightly floured work surface to about 1 cm/¹/₂ inch thick. Using a sharp knife, cut it into fingers and arrange on greased baking sheets, spaced slightly apart. Brush with the egg white.

❸ Bake in the preheated oven for 8–10 minutes, or until golden brown. Remove from the oven and leave to cool on the baking sheets. When completely cool, store in an airtight container, but they are best served as fresh as possible.

Quiche Lorraine

This elegant version of the classic French egg and bacon tart is delicious as it is, or it can form the basis of an even more elaborate quiche. You can, for example, arrange cooked or canned asparagus spears in a wheel on the top, or smother it with a layer of lightly sautéed mushrooms.

makes 1 x 23-cm/9-inch quiche

Pastry	Filling
175 g/6 oz plain flour, plus extra for dusting	115 g/4 oz Gruyère cheese, thinly sliced
pinch of salt	55 g/2 oz Roquefort cheese, crumbled
115 g/4 oz butter, diced	175 g/6 oz rindless lean bacon, grilled until crisp
25 g/1 oz pecorino cheese, grated	3 eggs
4–6 tbsp iced water	150 ml/5 fl oz double cream
	salt and pepper

Method

❶ To make the pastry, sift the flour with the salt into a bowl. Add the butter and rub it in with your fingertips until the mixture resembles breadcrumbs. Stir in the grated cheese, then stir in enough of the water to bind. Shape the dough into a ball, wrap in foil and chill in the refrigerator for 15 minutes.

❷ Preheat the oven to 190°C/375°F/Gas Mark 5. Unwrap and roll out the dough on a lightly floured work surface. Use to line a 23-cm/9-inch quiche tin. Place the tin on a baking sheet. Prick the base of the pastry case all over with a fork, line with foil or greaseproof paper and fill with baking beans. Bake in the preheated oven for 15 minutes, until the edges are set and dry.

Remove the beans and lining and bake the pastry case for a further 5–7 minutes, or until golden. Leave to cool slightly.

❸ For the filling, arrange both cheeses over the base of the pastry case, then crumble the bacon evenly on top. In a bowl, beat the eggs with the cream until thoroughly combined. Add salt and pepper to taste. Pour the mixture into the pastry case and return to the oven for 20 minutes, or until the filling is golden and set.

❹ Remove from the oven and cool the quiche in the tin for 10 minutes. Transfer to a wire rack to cool completely. Cover and store in the refrigerator, but return to room temperature before serving.

Moroccan Pickled Vegetables

Snacking is an art form in North Africa, so it is well worth adopting their clever ideas to serve as flavourful party food.

serves 12

225 g/8 oz small radishes

225 g/8 oz baby carrots

8 celery sticks

1 cucumber

salt and pepper

100 g/3½ oz caster sugar

125 ml/4 fl oz lemon juice

2 tbsp pink peppercorns

1 bunch of fresh coriander, finely chopped

Method

❶ Place the radishes and carrots in a large, non-metallic bowl. Cut the celery sticks into 5-cm/2-inch lengths and add to the bowl. Halve the cucumber lengthways, scoop out the seeds with a teaspoon and discard, then thickly slice and add to the bowl. Sprinkle the vegetables generously with salt, cover with clingfilm and leave to stand for 3–4 hours.

❷ Tip the vegetables into a colander and rinse thoroughly under cold running water to remove all traces of salt. Drain well and pat dry with kitchen paper. Transfer the vegetables to a non-metallic bowl.

❸ In a separate non-metallic bowl, mix together the sugar, lemon juice and peppercorns, stirring until the sugar has completely dissolved. Season to taste with pepper.

❹ Pour the dressing over the vegetables and toss gently to mix. Cover with clingfilm and chill for 8 hours or overnight in the refrigerator.

❺ Just before serving, stir in the chopped coriander, then transfer to a serving dish. Serve chilled with a supply of cocktail sticks for spearing the pickled vegetables.

Böreks

These crisp, cheese-filled pastries are a Turkish speciality, although they are popular throughout the Middle East. They are traditionally made with a ewe's milk cheese, but you could substitute grated Gruyère if you prefer.

makes 20

225 g/8 oz feta cheese (drained weight)

2 tbsp chopped fresh mint

2 tbsp chopped fresh parsley

1½ tbsp chopped fresh dill

pinch of freshly grated nutmeg

pepper

20 sheets filo pastry (about 12 x 18 cm/ 4½ x 7 inches), thawed if frozen

olive oil, for brushing

Method

❶ Preheat the oven to 190°C/375°F/ Gas Mark 5. Crumble the feta into a bowl and add the mint, parsley, dill and nutmeg. Season to taste with pepper and mix well.

❷ Keep the filo pastry sheets covered with clingfilm to prevent them drying out. Take a sheet of filo and brush with oil. Place a second sheet on top and brush with oil. Cut in half lengthways. Place a teaspoon of the cheese mixture at the short end of one long strip, fold in the corners

diagonally and roll up. Brush the end with a little oil to seal and place, seam side down, on a baking sheet. Repeat with the remaining sheets of filo and filling.

❸ Brush the tops of the pastries with a little more oil and bake in the preheated oven for 15–20 minutes, or until golden and crisp. Remove from the oven and transfer to a wire rack to cool. Serve at room temperature. The Böreks can also be deep-fried.

Little Feta & Spinach Crescents

The traditional recipe for spanakopita, a famous Greek pie, has been adapted to make these attractive, melt-in-the mouth crescents.

makes 16

450 g/1 lb spinach, thick stalks removed

4 spring onions, finely chopped

2 eggs, lightly beaten

1 tbsp chopped fresh parsley

1 tbsp chopped fresh dill

350 g/12 oz feta cheese (drained weight)

pepper

8 sheets filo pastry (about 12 x 18 cm/ 4½ x 7 inches), thawed if frozen

olive oil, for brushing

Method

❶ Preheat the oven to 190°C/375°F/Gas Mark 5. Pour water to a depth of about 1 cm/½ inch into a large saucepan and bring to the boil. Add the spinach and cook, turning once, for 1–2 minutes, until just wilted. Drain well, then squeeze out as much excess liquid as you can with your hands. Finely chop the spinach and place in a large bowl. Add the spring onions, eggs, parsley and dill. Crumble in the feta and season to taste with pepper. Mix together thoroughly.

❷ Keep the filo pastry sheets covered with clingfilm to prevent them drying out. Take a sheet of filo, brush with oil and cut in half lengthways. Spread a little of the filling across one corner, leaving a small margin on either side. Roll up securely but not too tightly and curl in the ends to make a crescent shape. Place on a baking sheet. Repeat with the remaining sheets of filo and filling.

❸ Brush the crescents with oil and bake in the preheated oven for 25 minutes, until golden and crisp. Remove from the oven and leave on the baking sheet for 5 minutes, then transfer to a wire rack to cool. Serve at room temperature.

Cheese & Apricot Morsels

These unusual little snacks make an eye-catching addition to a buffet table, yet are very easy and quick to make.

makes 20

225 g/8 oz cream cheese

6 tbsp milk

115 g/4 oz mature Cheddar cheese, finely grated

salt and pepper

800 g/1 lb 12 oz apricot halves, drained if canned

To garnish

about 20 walnut pieces

paprika

Method

❶ Beat the cream cheese in a bowl with a wooden spoon until softened. Gradually beat in the milk and Cheddar cheese. Season to taste with salt and pepper.

❷ Spoon the cheese mixture into a piping bag fitted with a 1-cm/½-inch star nozzle. Pipe swirls of the mixture into the hollow side of each apricot half.

❸ Arrange the filled apricot halves in a serving dish, then top each with a piece of walnut and dust lightly with a little paprika to garnish.

Caribbean Crab Cakes

These spicy snacks are delicious served warm as well as cold and go well with the Red Pepper Dip (see page 22) or Spicy Salsa (see page 78).

makes 16

1 potato, cut into chunks

pinch of salt

4 spring onions, chopped

1 garlic clove, chopped

1 tbsp chopped fresh thyme

1 tbsp chopped fresh basil

1 tbsp chopped fresh coriander

225 g/8 oz white crabmeat, drained if canned and thawed if frozen

½ tsp Dijon mustard

½ fresh green chilli, deseeded and finely chopped

1 egg, lightly beaten

pepper

plain flour, for dusting

sunflower oil, for frying

lime wedges, to garnish

dip or salsa of choice, to serve

Method

❶ Place the potato in a small saucepan and add water to cover. Add the salt. Bring to the boil, then reduce the heat, cover and simmer for 10–15 minutes, or until softened. Drain well, turn into a large bowl and mash with a potato masher or fork until smooth.

❷ Meanwhile, place the spring onions, garlic, thyme, basil and coriander in a mortar and pound with a pestle until smooth. Add the herb paste to the mashed potato with the crabmeat, mustard, chilli, egg and pepper to taste. Mix well, cover with clingfilm and chill in the refrigerator for 30 minutes.

❸ Sprinkle flour on to a shallow plate. Shape spoonfuls of the crabmeat mixture into small balls with your hands, then flatten slightly and dust with flour, shaking off any excess. Heat the oil in a frying pan over a high heat, add the crab cakes, in batches, and cook for 2–3 minutes on each side until golden. Remove from the frying pan and drain on kitchen paper. Leave to cool to room temperature.

❹ Arrange the crab cakes on a serving dish and garnish with lime wedges. Serve with a bowl of dip or salsa.

Anchovy, Olive &
Cheese Triangles

**Ideal for parties, these fabulous little Spanish tapas can be made in advance
and stored in an airtight container. If you can't find Manchego cheese,
substitute farmhouse Cheddar.**

makes 40

55 g/2 oz canned anchovy fillets in olive
oil, drained and roughly chopped

55 g/2 oz black olives, stoned and
roughly chopped

115 g/4 oz Manchego cheese, finely grated

115 g/4 oz plain flour, plus extra
for dusting

115 g/4 oz unsalted butter, diced

½ tsp cayenne pepper, plus extra
for dusting

Method

❶ Place the anchovies, olives, cheese,
flour, butter and cayenne pepper in a food
processor and pulse until a dough forms.
Turn out and shape into a ball. Wrap in foil
and chill in the refrigerator for 30 minutes.

❷ Preheat the oven to 200°C/400°F/Gas
Mark 6. Unwrap the dough, knead on a
lightly floured work surface and roll out
thinly. Using a sharp knife, cut it into strips
about 5 cm/2 inches wide. Cut diagonally
across each strip, turning the knife in
alternate directions, to make triangles.

❸ Arrange the triangles on 2 baking
sheets and dust lightly with cayenne
pepper. Bake in the preheated oven
for 10 minutes, or until golden brown.
Transfer to wire racks to cool completely.

Deep-fried Prawn Balls

These spicy Indonesian snacks are very moreish and are delicious served hot or cold. Sambal oelek is a fiery hot paste made from chillies. It is available from large supermarkets and Chinese food shops.

makes 25

280 g/10 oz raw prawns,
peeled and deveined
2.5-cm/1-inch piece fresh root ginger,
roughly chopped
225 g/8 oz beansprouts, roughly chopped
1 bunch of spring onions,
roughly chopped
115 g/4 oz plain flour

1 tsp baking powder
1 egg, lightly beaten
½ tsp sambal oelek
pinch of salt
1–2 tbsp lukewarm water (optional)
groundnut or sunflower oil,
for deep-frying
dip of choice, to serve (optional)

Method

❶ Place the prawns, ginger, beansprouts and spring onions in a food processor and process until finely chopped, scraping down the sides of the mixing bowl once or twice. Scrape the mixture into a bowl and add the flour, baking powder, egg, sambal oelek and salt. Mix thoroughly with your hands until a firm mixture forms, adding a little of the water if necessary.

❷ Heat the oil in a deep-fryer or large saucepan to 180–190°C/350–375°F, or until a cube of day-old bread browns in 30 seconds.

❸ Meanwhile, shape spoonfuls of the prawn mixture into walnut-sized balls with your hands. Add the prawn balls to the hot oil in batches, and deep-fry for 2–3 minutes, until golden brown. Remove with a slotted spoon and drain on kitchen paper. Leave to cool to room temperature before serving with a dip of your choice, if desired.

Sicilian Prawns

This attractive dish makes a lovely centrepiece for a buffet table, but you will need to provide plates and forks for your guests.

serves 12

500 g/1 lb 2 oz long-grain rice

3 tbsp white wine vinegar

1 tsp Dijon mustard

2 garlic cloves

150 ml/5 fl oz olive oil

salt and pepper

paprika

425 ml/15 fl oz mayonnaise

juice of 3 oranges

juice of ½ lemon

3 shallots, finely chopped

425 ml/15 fl oz passata

450 g/1 lb cooked peeled prawns

125 g/4½ oz flaked almonds

sunflower oil, for oiling

fresh parsley sprigs, to garnish

Method

❶ Bring a large saucepan of lightly salted water to the boil. Add the rice and return to the boil. Reduce the heat and simmer for 15 minutes, or until tender. Drain well, rinse under cold running water, then drain again and leave to cool completely.

❷ Mix the vinegar and mustard together in a non-metallic bowl. Place the garlic on a chopping board and smash with the side of a large, heavy knife. Sprinkle over a little salt and finely chop. Add the garlic to the vinegar mixture and mix, then gradually whisk in the oil until the dressing has thickened. Add salt and pepper to taste and lightly colour with paprika. Reserve.

❸ Mix the mayonnaise, orange juice, lemon juice, shallots and passata together in a separate non-metallic bowl. Fold in the prawns. Cover with clingfilm and chill in the refrigerator until required.

❹ When the rice is cold, add the dressing and stir in the almonds. Spoon the rice mixture into a lightly oiled round mould, cover with clingfilm and chill in the refrigerator for at least 30 minutes.

❺ To serve, turn out the rice on to a large serving plate, carefully scoop out the centre and spoon the prawn mixture into the hollow. Garnish with parsley sprigs.

Stuffed Vine Leaves

With all the sunny flavours of Greece, these vegetarian parcels are perfect for a summer party.

serves 12

350 g/12 oz long-grain rice

450 g/1 lb vine leaves, fresh or preserved in brine

2 onions, finely chopped

1 bunch of spring onions, finely chopped

1 bunch of fresh parsley, finely chopped

25 g/1 oz fresh mint, finely chopped

1 tbsp fennel seeds

1 tsp crushed dried chillies

finely grated rind of 2 lemons

225 ml/8 fl oz olive oil

salt

600 ml/1 pint boiling water

lemon wedges, to garnish

Tzatziki (see page 16), to serve

Method

❶ Bring a large saucepan of lightly salted water to the boil. Add the rice and boil return to the boil. Reduce the heat and simmer for 15 minutes, or until tender.

❷ Meanwhile, if using preserved vine leaves, rinse and place them in a heatproof bowl and pour over boiling water to cover. Leave to soak for 10 minutes. If using fresh vine leaves, bring a saucepan of water to the boil, add the vine leaves, then reduce the heat and simmer for 10 minutes.

❸ Drain the rice and mix with the onions, spring onions, parsley, mint, fennel seeds, chillies, lemon rind and 3 tablespoons of the oil in a large bowl. Season with salt.

❹ Drain the vine leaves well. Spread out 1 leaf, vein side up, on a work surface.

Place a generous teaspoonful of the rice mixture on the leaf near the stalk. Fold the stalk end over the filling, fold in the sides and roll up the leaf. Repeat until all the filling has been used. Use any leftover vine leaves to line a serving platter, if desired.

❺ Place the parcels in a large, heavy-based saucepan in a single layer (you may need to use 2 pans). Spoon over the remaining oil, then add the boiling water. Cover the parcels with an inverted heatproof plate to keep them below the surface of the water, cover the pan and simmer for 1 hour.

❻ Allow the parcels to cool to room temperature in the saucepan, then transfer to a serving platter with a slotted spoon. Garnish with lemon wedges and serve with Tzatziki.

Vegetable Samosas

These aromatic Indian snacks are always popular and taste good served hot or cold. You can make them in advance and freeze them ready to cook or to serve after thawing.

makes 30

3 large potatoes, cut into chunks

salt

85 g/3 oz frozen peas

55 g/2 oz frozen sweetcorn kernels, thawed

2 shallots, finely chopped

1 tsp ground cumin

1 tsp ground coriander

2 fresh green chillies, deseeded and finely chopped

2 tbsp chopped fresh mint

2 tbsp chopped fresh coriander

4 tbsp lemon juice

15 sheets filo pastry (about 12 x 18 cm/ 4½ x 7 inches), thawed if frozen

melted butter, for brushing

groundnut or sunflower oil, for deep-frying

mango chutney, to serve

Method

❶ Place the potatoes in a saucepan and add cold water to cover and a pinch of salt. Bring to the boil, then reduce the heat, cover and simmer for 15–20 minutes, until tender. Meanwhile, cook the peas according to the instructions on the packet. Drain and transfer to a bowl. Drain the potatoes, return to the saucepan and mash coarsely with a potato masher or fork. Add them to the peas.

❷ Add the sweetcorn, shallots, cumin, ground coriander, chillies, mint, fresh coriander and lemon juice and season to taste with salt. Mix well.

❸ Keep the filo pastry sheets covered with clingfilm to prevent them drying out.

Take a sheet of filo, brush with melted butter and cut in half lengthways. Place a tablespoonful of the filling at one end of a strip. Fold over a corner to make a triangle and roll up the pastry strip. Repeat with the remaining sheets of filo and filling.

❹ Heat the oil in a deep-fryer or large saucepan to 180–190°C/350–375°F, or until a cube of day-old bread browns in 30 seconds. Add the samosas in batches, and cook until golden brown. Remove with a slotted spoon and drain on kitchen paper. Alternatively, bake the samosas in a preheated oven, 200°C/400°F/Gas Mark 6, for 10–15 minutes, until golden brown. Serve hot or at room temperature with mango chutney.

Sausage Rolls

Home-made sausage rolls are so much tastier than the shop-bought variety, especially if you can buy good-quality sausagemeat. They are very easy to make and can be served warm or cold.

makes 48

450 g/1 lb sausagemeat

1 tsp Worcestershire sauce

beaten egg, to glaze

Pastry

225 g/8 oz plain flour, plus extra for dusting

pinch of salt

½ tsp mustard powder

115 g/4 oz butter, diced

2–3 tbsp iced water

Method

❶ For the pastry, sift the flour into a bowl with the salt and mustard powder. Add the butter and rub it in with your fingertips until the mixture resembles breadcrumbs. Gradually stir in enough of the water to make a soft, but not sticky, dough. Shape the dough into a ball, wrap in foil and chill in the refrigerator for 20 minutes.

❷ Preheat the oven to 190°C/375°F/ Gas Mark 5. Mix the sausagemeat and Worcestershire sauce together in a bowl until thoroughly combined and the meat is broken up. Divide the mixture into 12 portions and roll each one between the palms of your hands to make a 15-cm/ 6-inch long sausage.

❸ Roll out the dough on a lightly floured work surface to a rectangle measuring 20 x 46 cm/8 x 18 inches. Using a sharp knife, cut the dough into 12 rectangles, each measuring about 5 x 15 cm/ 2 x 6 inches. Place a sausage-meat roll on a dough rectangle and brush the long edges of the dough with water. Roll the pastry over the sausagemeat to enclose it, then cut the roll into 4 equal pieces. Repeat with the remaining dough and sausagemeat rolls.

❹ Arrange the sausage rolls on 2 baking sheets, seam-side down. Brush with the beaten egg and bake in the preheated oven for 10 minutes, or until golden brown and cooked through. Remove from the oven and transfer the sausage rolls to a wire rack to cool.

Honey & Mustard Drumsticks

Chicken drumsticks make good party food as they are so easy to eat with the fingers. This sweet and sour marinade makes them completely irresistible.

makes 12

12 chicken drumsticks

175 ml/6 fl oz clear honey

6 tbsp wholegrain mustard

2 tbsp Dijon mustard

2 tbsp white wine vinegar

3 tbsp sunflower oil

fresh parsley sprigs, to garnish

Method

❶ Using a sharp knife, make several slashes in each drumstick, then place them in a large, non-metallic dish.

❷ Mix the honey, both types of mustard, vinegar and oil together in a jug, whisking well to combine. Pour the marinade over the chicken, turning and stirring to coat. Cover with clingfilm and set aside in the refrigerator to marinate for at least 2–3 hours, or overnight.

❸ Preheat the grill to medium. Drain the chicken drumsticks, reserving the marinade. Place the drumsticks on a grill rack and cook under the hot grill, turning and brushing frequently with the marinade, for 25 minutes, or until the chicken is tender and the juices run clear when a skewer is inserted into the thickest part of the meat. Leave to cool, then arrange on a serving platter and garnish with parsley sprigs.

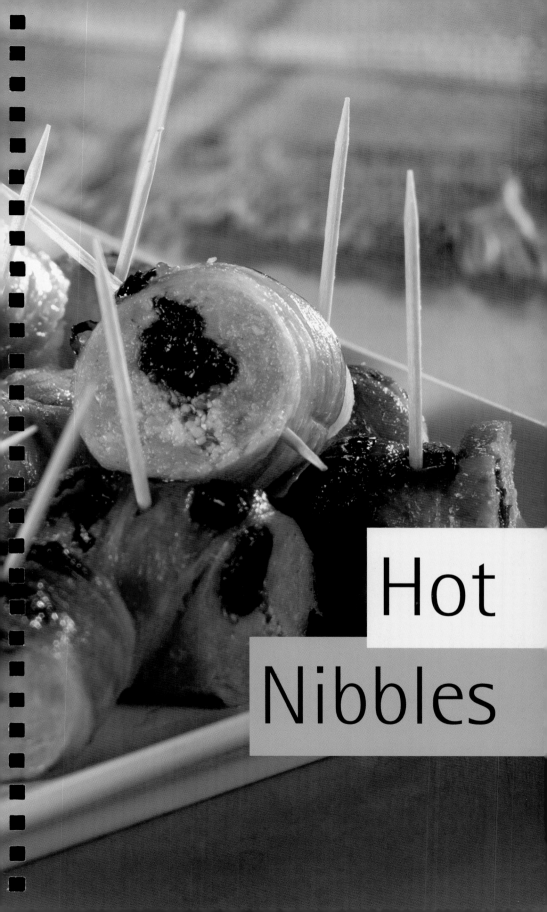

Hot
Nibbles

Spicy Seafood Kebabs

These tempting prawn and monkfish skewers are perfect for parties because they take only a few minutes to cook.

makes 8

2 tsp grated fresh root ginger

2 garlic cloves, finely chopped

2 fresh green chillies, deseeded and finely chopped

2 tbsp groundnut or sunflower oil

1.5 kg/3 lb 5 oz monkfish fillet, cut into 24 chunks

8 raw tiger prawns, peeled and tails left intact

Spicy salsa

2 tomatoes

4 fresh Scotch bonnet chillies

4 fresh green jalapeño chillies, deseeded and finely chopped

2 tbsp chopped fresh coriander

2 tbsp olive oil

1 tbsp red wine vinegar

salt and pepper

Method

❶ Mix the ginger, garlic, green chillies and oil together in a large, non-metallic bowl. Add the monkfish chunks and prawns and stir well to coat. Cover and leave to marinate in the refrigerator for 1 hour.

❷ Preheat the grill to medium. To make the salsa, cut a small cross in the bottom of each tomato, place in a heatproof bowl and pour over boiling water to cover. Leave for 30 seconds until the skins begin to peel back. Drain and, when cool enough to handle, peel.

❸ Place the Scotch bonnet chillies on a baking sheet and cook under the hot grill, turning frequently, until the skin blackens and blisters. Using tongs, transfer to a polythene bag and tie the top.

❹ Place the jalapeño chillies in a bowl. Scoop out and discard the tomato seeds, finely chop the flesh and add to the bowl. Remove the Scotch bonnet chillies from the bag and peel away the skins. Halve them, discard the seeds and finely chop the flesh. (Wear rubber gloves to protect your hands as they are very hot.) Add them to the bowl with the coriander. Whisk the oil with the vinegar in a small bowl and season to taste with salt. Pour over the salsa, cover with clingfilm and chill in the refrigerator until required.

❺ Thread the seafood on to 8 presoaked wooden skewers. Cook under the hot grill, turning frequently, for 6–8 minutes, until cooked and tender. Transfer to a serving dish, season and serve with the salsa.

Seafood Filo Parcels

These decorative, crisp filo pastry parcels are filled with succulent salmon and tasty crabmeat.

makes 24

100 g/3½ oz canned red salmon, drained

100 g/3½ oz canned crabmeat, drained

2 tbsp chopped fresh parsley

8 spring onions, finely chopped

8 sheets filo pastry (about 20 x 30 cm/ 8 x 12 inches), thawed if frozen

melted butter, for brushing

sunflower oil, for oiling

Method

❶ Preheat the oven to 200°C/400°F/Gas Mark 6. Remove and discard the skin and bones from the salmon, place in a bowl and flake the flesh with a fork. Remove and discard any cartilage from the crabmeat, place in another bowl and flake with a fork. Divide the parsley and spring onions between the bowls and mix well.

❷ Keep the filo pastry sheets covered with clingfilm to prevent them drying out. Take a sheet of filo, brush with melted butter, then place a second sheet on top. Cut into 10-cm/4-inch squares. Place a teaspoonful of the salmon mixture on each square. Brush the edges of the pastry with melted butter, then draw together to make little pouches. Press to seal. Repeat with 2 more sheets of filo and the salmon mixture, then repeat with the remaining sheets of filo and the crabmeat mixture.

❸ Lightly oil a baking sheet and place the parcels on it. Bake in the preheated oven for 15 minutes, until the pastry is golden. Serve warm.

Devils & Angels on Horseback

Tempting morsels to bring out the devil in you and raise the party spirit, these are delicious, classic snacks on a stick.

makes 32

Devils	Angels
8 rindless lean bacon rashers	8 rindless lean bacon rashers
8 canned anchovy fillets, drained	16 smoked oysters, drained if canned
16 blanched almonds	
16 no-soak prunes	

Method

❶ Preheat the oven to 200°C/400°F/Gas Mark 6. For the Devils, cut each bacon rasher lengthways in half and gently stretch with the back of a knife. Cut each anchovy fillet lengthways in half. Wrap an anchovy half around each almond and press them into the cavity where the stones have been removed from the prunes. Wrap a strip of bacon around each prune and secure with a cocktail stick.

❷ For the Angels, cut each bacon rasher lengthways in half and gently stretch with the back of a knife. Wrap a bacon strip around each oyster and secure with a cocktail stick.

❸ Place the Devils and Angels on a baking sheet and cook in the preheated oven for 10–15 minutes, until sizzling hot and the bacon is cooked. Serve hot.

San Francisco Wings

Chicken wings cooked in a wonderfully sticky, slightly spicy sauce never fail to please. You can serve the wings hot or warm.

makes 12

5 tbsp dark soy sauce

2 tbsp dry sherry

1 tbsp rice vinegar

5-cm/2-inch strip of orange rind, pith removed

juice of 1 orange

1 tbsp light muscovado sugar

1 star anise

1 tsp cornflour, mixed to a paste with 3 tbsp water

1 tbsp finely chopped fresh root ginger

1 tsp chilli sauce

1.5 kg/3 lb 5 oz chicken wings

Method

❶ Preheat the oven to 200°C/400°F/Gas Mark 6. Place the soy sauce, sherry, vinegar, orange rind, orange juice, sugar and star anise in a saucepan and mix well. Bring to the boil over a medium heat, then stir in the cornflour paste. Continue to boil, stirring constantly, for 1 minute, or until thickened. Remove the pan from the heat and stir in the ginger and chilli sauce.

❷ Remove and discard the tips from the chicken wings and place the wings in a single layer in an ovenproof dish or roasting tin. Pour the sauce over the wings, turning and stirring to coat.

❸ Bake in the preheated oven for 35–40 minutes, turning and basting with the sauce occasionally, until the chicken is tender and browned and the juices run clear when a skewer is inserted into the thickest part of the meat. Serve either hot or warm.

Spare Ribs

Terrific to eat but astonishingly messy, so provide plenty of paper napkins. Sticky ribs are easy to prepare and won't keep you away from your guests for long.

makes 30

2 tbsp groundnut or sunflower oil

1 onion, chopped

1 garlic clove, finely chopped

1 fresh green chilli, deseeded and finely chopped

3 tbsp clear honey

2 tbsp tomato purée

1 tbsp white wine vinegar

pinch of chilli powder

150 ml/5 fl oz chicken stock

800 g/1 lb 12 oz pork spare ribs

Method

❶ Preheat the oven to 190°C/375°F/Gas Mark 5. Heat the oil in a heavy-based saucepan over a medium heat. Add the onion, garlic and chilli and cook, stirring occasionally, for 5 minutes, until softened. Stir in the honey, tomato purée, white wine vinegar, chilli powder and stock and bring to the boil. Reduce the heat and simmer, stirring occasionally, for 15 minutes, until the sauce has thickened.

❷ Meanwhile, chop the spare ribs into 5-cm/2-inch lengths and place in a roasting tin. Pour the sauce over them, turning and stirring to coat. Roast in the preheated oven for 1 hour, turning and basting with the sauce frequently, until the ribs are thoroughly browned and sticky.

❸ Remove from the oven and transfer to a warm serving dish. Serve immediately.

Indonesian Peanut Fritters

These crisp bites are so effortless that you can cook them when the party is in full swing. Equally, you can prepare them in advance and quickly reheat in the oven when required.

makes 20

55 g/2 oz rice flour

½ tsp baking powder

½ tsp ground turmeric

½ tsp ground coriander

¼ tsp ground cumin

1 garlic clove, finely chopped

55 g/2 oz unsalted peanuts, crushed

125–150 ml/4–5 fl oz coconut milk

salt

groundnut oil, for frying

Method

❶ Combine the rice flour, baking powder, turmeric, coriander, cumin, garlic and peanuts in a bowl. Gradually stir in enough coconut milk to make a smooth, thin batter. Season to taste with salt.

❷ Pour the oil into a heavy-based frying pan to a depth of about 1 cm/½ inch and heat over a high heat until hot. Add tablespoonfuls of the batter to the pan, spacing them well apart, and fry until the tops have just set and the undersides are golden. Turn the fritters over and cook for 1 minute, until the second side is golden. Remove with a fish slice, drain on kitchen paper and keep warm while you cook the remaining fritters. Serve immediately.

❸ Alternatively, transfer the fritters to wire racks to cool, then store in an airtight container. When ready to serve, preheat the oven to 180°C/350°F/Gas Mark 4. Place the fritters on baking sheets and reheat in the oven for 10 minutes.

Mini Pepperoni Pizzas

Pizzas are always a firm favourite with party guests, and the scone base used here is much quicker and easier to make than a traditional bread dough base.

makes 12

Bases	Pepperoni topping
525 g/1 lb 3 oz self-raising flour, plus extra for dusting	175 ml/6 fl oz ready-made tomato pizza sauce
1 tsp salt	115 g/4 oz rindless smoked bacon, diced
85 g/3 oz butter, diced	1 orange pepper, deseeded and chopped
300–350 ml/10–12 fl oz milk	85 g/3 oz pepperoni sausage, sliced
olive oil, for oiling	55 g/2 oz mozzarella cheese, grated
	½ tsp dried oregano
	olive oil, for drizzling
	salt and pepper

Method

❶ Preheat the oven to 200°C/400°F/Gas Mark 6. To make the bases, sift the flour and salt into a bowl, add the butter and rub it in with your fingertips until the mixture resembles breadcrumbs. Make a well in the centre of the mixture and add 300 ml/10 fl oz of the milk. Mix with the blade of a knife to a soft dough, adding the remaining milk if necessary.

❷ Turn out on to a lightly floured work surface and knead gently. Divide the dough into 12 equal pieces and roll out each piece into a round. Place on a lightly oiled baking sheet and gently push up the edges of each pizza to form a rim.

❸ For the topping, spread the tomato sauce over the bases almost to the edge. Arrange the bacon, orange pepper and pepperoni on top and sprinkle with the cheese. Sprinkle with the oregano, drizzle with a little oil and season to taste with salt and pepper.

❹ Bake in the preheated oven for 10–15 minutes, or until the edges are crisp and the cheese is bubbling. Serve.

Mini Artichoke Pizzas

This recipe offers an alternative, equally tempting topping for the simple scone base featured on page 90. Make a mixed batch for a colourful addition to your party buffet.

makes 12

Bases	Artichoke topping
525 g/1 lb 3 oz self-raising flour, plus extra for dusting	175 ml/6 fl oz ready-made tomato pizza sauce
1 tsp salt	55 g/2 oz dolcelatte cheese, sliced
85 g/3 oz butter, diced	115 g/4 oz canned artichoke hearts in oil, drained and sliced
300–350 ml/10–12 fl oz milk	2 shallots, chopped
olive oil, for oiling	55 g/2 oz Gruyère cheese, grated
	4 tbsp freshly grated Parmesan cheese
	½ tsp dried oregano
	olive oil, for drizzling
	salt and pepper

Method

❶ Preheat the oven to 200°C/400°F/Gas Mark 6. To prepare the bases, follow Steps 1 and 2 on page 90.

❷ For the topping, spread the tomato sauce over the bases almost to the edge. Arrange the dolcelatte slices, artichoke hearts and shallots on top. Mix together the Gruyère and Parmesan in a bowl and sprinkle over the pizzas. Sprinkle with the oregano, drizzle with oil and season to taste with salt and pepper.

❸ Bake in the preheated oven for 10–15 minutes, or until the edges are crisp and the cheese is bubbling. Serve.

Bruschetta

These savoury Italian toasts taste terrific and can be prepared in advance, ready to pop in the oven when your guests arrive.

makes 30

3 thin ciabatta loaves or baguettes

125 ml/4 fl oz green pesto or

125 ml/4 fl oz red pesto

450 g/1 lb mozzarella cheese, diced

2 tsp dried oregano

pepper

3 tbsp olive oil

Method

❶ Preheat the oven to 220°C/425°F/Gas Mark 7 and preheat the grill to medium. Slice the loaves diagonally and discard the crusty ends. Toast the slices on both sides under the hot grill until golden.

❷ Spread one side of each slice of toast with either green or red pesto and top with the mozzarella. Sprinkle with the oregano and season to taste with pepper.

❸ Place the bruschetta on a large baking sheet and drizzle with the oil. Bake in the preheated oven for 5 minutes, or until the cheese has melted and is bubbling. Remove the bruschetta from the oven and leave for 5 minutes before serving.

Pigs in Blankets

This is a more interesting version of the ever-popular sausages on sticks. For extra variety, use a mixture of differently flavoured sausages.

makes 48

16 large, good-quality sausages

4 tbsp Dijon mustard

48 no-soak prunes

16 rindless smoked bacon rashers

Method

❶ Preheat the grill to medium. Cut a deep slit along the length of each sausage without cutting all the way through. Spread the mustard evenly over the cut sides of the slits. Place 3 prunes inside each slit, pressing the sausages together.

❷ Gently stretch each bacon rasher with the back of a knife. Wind a rasher around each sausage to hold it together.

❸ Cook under the hot grill, turning frequently, for 15 minutes, or until cooked through. Transfer to a chopping board and cut each 'pig' into 3 pieces, each containing a prune. Spear with cocktail sticks, arrange on a plate and serve.

Barbecue Food

Cooking food outdoors on a barbecue is great fun and a delicious way of feeding a crowd. To keep everybody happy, it is always a good idea to offer a range of meat and seafood dishes, vegetables, salads and desserts, so that there is something for meat-eaters, vegetarians and even fussy children.

The dishes can be as straightforward or complicated as you wish. You can start by

cooking a basic barbecue with traditional ingredients such as sausages, burgers, chicken drumsticks, chops and steaks. Served with burger buns, French bread or baked potatoes and plenty of fresh leafy or mixed salad, good food doesn't get much easier.

Once you have got the hang of cooking on your barbecue, you can experiment with more elaborate dishes. Thread seafood, poultry, vegetables or fruit on to wooden skewers to make kebabs. Add extra flavour and succulence to the food by mixing various marinades and dressings.

The key to a successful barbecue is good planning. It helps to know roughly how many people are coming. If the numbers are very vague or large, you need to lay on a plentiful supply of

basics, such as burgers, salad and bread, so that nobody goes hungry. Reserve supplies can be kept in the refrigerator and frozen later if not needed.

To cater for vegetarian guests, prepare plenty of vegetable kebabs and parcels which others can eat, too. Offer different fillings to go with baked potatoes: a creamy cheese or a spicy sweetcorn relish are very popular. A good selection of colourful salads, including a pasta, rice, tomato or mixed bean salad, will please vegetarians but appeal to everyone else as well.

Before you start a barbecue party, you should consider the safety aspects – barbecuing is a safe way of cooking as long as you take a few sensible precautions.

• Position your barbecue away from overhanging trees and shrubs to avoid branches catching fire. Have a bucket of water nearby in case the fire blows out of control.

• Trim off excess fat and shake away surplus marinade before putting the food on the barbecue to stop fat dripping down on to the hot coals and bursting into flames.

• To minimize the risk of food poisoning, make sure that meat and seafood are cooked through. Test the meat by piercing it with a skewer or the tip of a sharp knife – it is cooked when the juices run clear (not pink). Once it has cooled down, never return poultry to the grill to finish cooking.

• Keep salads and cooked foods away from raw

meat. Use different chopping boards, utensils, tea towels and plates for dealing with raw and cooked meats or salad ingredients.

• On hot days, store foods out of direct sunlight and keep them chilled for as long as possible before cooking or serving. Cover food with netting or clean tea towels to keep insects off.

• Never leave the barbecue unattended. Warn any small children to keep away from the hot fire. Ban pets from the food and cooking areas as well, to prevent contamination and accidents.

• Use long-handled utensils and oven gloves to avoid getting burned and splashed.

• The person cooking should go easy on the alcohol. Discourage other adults who have been drinking from cooking, too.

Types of Fuel

There are many different types of fuel, and an equally wide range of barbecues, so consider your exact requirements before spending any money.

• Lumpwood charcoal is readily available, inexpensive and easy to light, but burns quickly.

• Charcoal briquettes take longer to catch, but burn for a long time and produce little smoke.

• Self-igniting charcoal is lumpwood charcoal or charcoal briquettes that have been coated with a flammable chemical. They light easily but you cannot start cooking until the chemical has burnt off as it can taint the food.

• Wood fires need constant attention. Hardwoods, such as mesquite, oak and apple, are best as they burn slowly and have a pleasant smell. Softwoods, however, burn too fast and tend to spark.

• Wood chips and herbs, such as sprigs of thyme or rosemary, can be sprinkled on the fire to give off a delicious aroma.

Choosing your Barbecue

Before buying a barbecue, consider the number of people you will want to feed; how often you are likely to use it; how it will fit into your garden, if you need one that is portable and how much you are prepared to spend on it.

• Disposable barbecues are inexpensive foil trays with enough fuel to burn for about one hour – ideal for a small, one-off picnic.

• Hibachi or 'firebox' barbecues from Japan are small, lightweight, reusable and easy to transport.

• Portable barbecues are light and easy to fold up and carry in the boot of a car for larger picnics.

• Brazier barbecues can be moved about the garden and stored easily. Some are a little low so check that the one you are thinking of buying is a comfortable height for the person who will be doing most of the cooking. If your garden is windy, choose a barbecue with a hood to protect the open grill.

• Kettle-grill barbecues are the next best thing to a permanent barbecue. The lid covers the grill and can save a barbecue party if it starts to rain. Many have a spit-roast for cooking chickens and joints.

• Gas and electric barbecues are expensive but easy to operate and very quick – they only take ten minutes to warm up. However, they do not give the food the traditional smoky flavour it gets from being cooked over charcoal.

• Permanent, tailor-made barbecues are an excellent choice if you barbecue frequently. You can buy kits or use simple materials such as house bricks and firebricks to build a fireplace and fit an adjustable metal rack.

Preparation

It is possible to make some dishes for your barbecue, such as meat kebabs, well in advance and freeze them—all you have to do is take them out the night before and thaw them thoroughly. Alternatively, you can make them the previous day and store them in the refrigerator overnight. You may also start marinating food the day before.

Leave the chopping and mixing of any salad ingredients until the morning of the barbecue. Toss in the dressing just before you are ready to serve them, so that the leaves and other ingredients do not go limp and soggy.

Hints & Tips

• Remember to light your barbecue at least an hour before you want to start cooking, to make sure it will be hot. For setting the fire, follow the instructions that come with the fuel you are using.

• To ensure even and thorough cooking, do not place too much food on the grill rack at once.

• To avoid contamination, aim to cook the same types of food together. Do not mix meat, fish and vegetarian dishes on the grill. The best plan is to wrap the vegetarian ingredients in foil parcels.

• Foil-wrapped potatoes work well, especially if you bake them in a conventional oven at 200°C/400°F/Gas Mark 6 for 30 minutes before moving them to the barbecue to finish cooking.

• Foil parcels are often the best solution for hot desserts. Just wrap the fruit and leave it to cook around the edge of the grill where the temperature is slightly lower.

• Offer a choice of drinks, both alcoholic and non-alcoholic: a fruit punch is usually popular.

• Even when rain stops play, you can keep cooking if you shut the lid of your barbecue and open the vents. Alternatively, you can take the food inside and carry on cooking under the grill in your kitchen. When the sun comes out again you can move back into the garden.

Meat
& Poultry

Tabasco Steaks with Watercress Butter

A variation on a classic theme, this simple but rather extravagant dish is ideal for a special occasion barbecue party.

serves 4

1 bunch of watercress

85 g/3 oz unsalted butter, softened

4 sirloin steaks, about 225 g/8 oz each

4 tsp Tabasco sauce

salt and pepper

Method

❶ Preheat the barbecue. Using a sharp knife, finely chop enough watercress to fill 4 tablespoons. Reserve a few watercress leaves for the garnish. Place the butter in a small bowl and beat in the chopped watercress with a fork until fully incorporated. Cover with clingfilm and leave to chill in the refrigerator until required.

❷ Sprinkle each steak with 1 teaspoon of the Tabasco sauce, rubbing it in well. Season to taste with salt and pepper.

❸ Cook the steaks over hot coals, 2½ minutes each side for rare, 4 minutes each side for medium and 6 minutes each side for well done. Transfer to serving plates, garnish with the reserved watercress leaves and serve immediately, topped with the watercress butter.

Variation

If you prefer, substitute the same amount of fresh parsley for the watercress.

Best Ever Burgers

Barbecues and burgers are almost inseparable. However, these succulent, home-made burgers bear no resemblance to the little ready-made patties available in most shops.

serves 6

900 g/2 lb lean minced steak

2 onions, finely chopped

25 g/1 oz fresh white breadcrumbs

1 egg, lightly beaten

1½ teaspoons finely chopped fresh thyme

salt and pepper

To serve

6 sesame seed baps

2 tomatoes

1 onion

lettuce leaves

mayonnaise

mustard

tomato ketchup

Method

❶ Preheat the barbecue. Place the steak, onions, breadcrumbs, egg and thyme in a large glass bowl and season to taste with salt and pepper. Mix thoroughly using your hands.

❷ Form the mixture into 6 large patties with your hands, neatening the edges with a round-bladed knife.

❸ Cook the burgers over hot coals for 3–4 minutes on each side. Meanwhile, cut the baps in half and briefly toast on the barbecue, cut-side down. Using a sharp knife, slice the tomatoes and cut the onion into thinly sliced rings. Fill the toasted baps with the cooked burgers, lettuce, sliced tomatoes and onion rings and serve immediately, with the mayonnaise, mustard and tomato ketchup.

Variation

For Tex-Mex burgers, add 2 deseeded and finely chopped fresh green chillies to the mixture in Step 1 and serve with Guacamole (see page 20).

Luxury Cheeseburgers

This is a sophisticated version of the traditional burger with a surprise filling of melted blue cheese. Serve with plenty of salad leaves to make a substantial barbecue lunch.

serves 4

55 g/2 oz Stilton cheese
450 g/1 lb lean minced steak
1 onion, finely chopped
1 celery stick, finely chopped
1 tsp creamed horseradish
1 tbsp chopped fresh thyme
salt and pepper

To serve
4 sesame seed baps
lettuce leaves
sliced tomatoes

Method

❶ Preheat the barbecue. Crumble the cheese into a bowl and reserve until required. Place the steak, onion, celery, horseradish and thyme in a separate bowl and season to taste with salt and pepper. Mix thoroughly using your hands.

❷ Form the mixture into 8 patties with your hands and a round-bladed knife. Divide the cheese between 4 of them and top with the remaining patties. Gently press them together and mould the edges.

❸ Cook the burgers over hot coals for 5 minutes on each side. Meanwhile, cut the baps in half and briefly toast on the barbecue, cut-side down. Fill the baps with the cooked burgers, lettuce and tomato slices and serve immediately.

Variation

Substitute Wensleydale or Lancashire cheese for the Stilton cheese and finely snipped chives for the thyme.

Rack & Ruin

This quick and easy dish is perfect for serving as part of a summer party menu, along with plenty of salad and potatoes.

serves 4

4 racks of lamb, each with 4 cutlets

2 tbsp extra virgin olive oil

1 tbsp balsamic vinegar

1 tbsp lemon juice

3 tbsp finely chopped fresh rosemary

1 small onion, finely chopped

salt and pepper

Method

❶ Place the racks of lamb in a large, shallow, non-metallic dish. Make a marinade by placing the oil, vinegar, lemon juice, rosemary and onion in a jug and stirring together. Season to taste with salt and pepper.

❷ Pour the marinade over the lamb and turn until thoroughly coated. Cover with clingfilm and marinate in the refrigerator for 1 hour, turning occasionally.

❸ Preheat the barbecue. Drain the racks of lamb, reserving the marinade. Cook over medium-hot coals, brushing frequently with the marinade, for 10 minutes on each side. Serve immediately.

Minted Lamb Steaks

You can prepare this dish with any kind of lamb chops – leg chops are especially tender – or cutlets, in which case you will probably require two per serving. Shoulder steaks also work well.

serves 6

6 chump chops, about 175 g/6 oz each

150 ml/5 fl oz natural Greek yogurt

2 garlic cloves, finely chopped

1 tsp grated fresh root ginger

1/4 tsp coriander seeds, crushed

salt and pepper

1 tbsp olive oil, plus extra for brushing

1 tbsp orange juice

1 tsp walnut oil

2 tbsp chopped fresh mint

Method

❶ Place the chops in a large, shallow, non-metallic bowl. Mix half the yogurt, the garlic, ginger and coriander seeds together in a jug and season to taste with salt and pepper. Spoon the mixture over the chops, turning to coat them evenly, then cover with clingfilm and leave to marinate in the refrigerator for 2 hours, turning occasionally.

❷ Preheat the barbecue. Place the remaining yogurt, the olive oil, orange juice, walnut oil and mint in a small bowl and, using a hand-held whisk, whisk until thoroughly blended. Season to taste with salt and pepper. Cover the minted yogurt with clingfilm and leave to chill in the refrigerator until ready to serve.

❸ Drain the chops, scraping off the marinade. Brush with olive oil and cook over medium-hot coals for 5–7 minutes on each side. Serve immediately with the minted yogurt.

Variation

If you prefer, omit the orange juice and walnut oil and stir in 1/4 teaspoon ground star anise and a pinch each of ground cinnamon and ground cumin.

Normandy Brochettes

The orchards of Normandy are famous throughout France, providing both eating apples and cider-making varieties. For an authentic touch, enjoy a glass of Calvados between courses.

serves 4

450 g/1 lb pork fillet	6 black peppercorns, crushed
300 ml/10 fl oz dry cider	2 crisp eating apples
1 tbsp finely chopped fresh sage	1 tbsp sunflower oil

Method

❶ Using a sharp knife, cut the pork into 2.5-cm/1-inch cubes, then place in a large, shallow, non-metallic dish. Mix the cider, sage and peppercorns together in a jug, pour the mixture over the pork and turn until thoroughly coated. Cover with clingfilm and leave to marinate in the refrigerator for 1–2 hours.

❷ Preheat the barbecue. Drain the pork, reserving the marinade. Core the apples, but do not peel them, then cut into wedges. Dip the apple wedges into the reserved marinade and thread on to several metal skewers, alternating with the cubes of pork. Stir the oil into the remaining marinade.

❸ Cook the brochettes over medium-hot coals, turning and brushing frequently with the reserved marinade, for 12–15 minutes. Transfer to a large serving plate and, if you prefer, remove the meat and apples from the skewers before serving. Serve immediately.

Variation

Replace 1 apple with 6 no-soak dried prunes wrapped in strips of streaky bacon. Thread the prunes on to the skewers with the remaining apple and pork.

Sausages with Barbecue Sauce

Although there is much more to barbecues than sausages, they can make a welcome appearance from time to time. This delicious sauce is a wonderful excuse for including them.

serves 4

2 tbsp sunflower oil	4 tbsp white wine vinegar
1 large onion, chopped	½ tsp mild chilli powder
2 garlic cloves, chopped	¼ tsp mustard powder
225 g/8 oz canned chopped tomatoes	dash of Tabasco sauce
1 tbsp Worcestershire sauce	salt and pepper
2 tbsp brown fruity sauce	450 g/1 lb sausages
2 tbsp light muscovado sugar	bread finger rolls, to serve

Method

❶ Preheat the barbecue. To make the sauce, heat the oil in a saucepan and fry the onion and garlic for 4–5 minutes, until softened and just beginning to brown.

❷ Add the tomatoes, Worcestershire sauce, brown fruity sauce, sugar, white wine vinegar, chilli powder, mustard powder and Tabasco sauce to the saucepan. Add salt and pepper to taste, and bring to the boil.

❸ Reduce the heat and simmer gently for 10–15 minutes, until the sauce begins to thicken slightly, stirring occasionally. Set aside and keep warm until required.

❹ Cook the sausages over hot coals for 10–15 minutes, turning frequently. Do not prick them with a fork or the juices and fat will run out and cause the barbecue to flare.

❺ Insert the sausages into the bread rolls and serve with the barbecue sauce.

Variation

Lincolnshire sausages have a good flavour. Cumberland sausages are tasty and also available in a coil (secure the coil with skewers as it cooks). Venison sausages have a gamey flavour and are good for barbecues.

Meatballs on Sticks

These are popular with children and adults alike. Serve with a selection
of ready-made or home-made sauces, such as a tomato relish,
heated on the side of the barbecue, or Spicy Salsa (see page 78).

serves 8

4 pork and herb sausages

115 g/4 oz fresh beef mince

85 g/3 oz fresh white breadcrumbs

1 onion, finely chopped

2 tbsp chopped mixed fresh herbs, such as
parsley, thyme and sage

1 egg

salt and pepper

sunflower oil, for brushing

sauces of your choice, to serve

Method

❶ Preheat the barbecue. Remove the
sausagemeat from the skins, place in a
large bowl and break up with a fork. Add
the beef mince, breadcrumbs, onion, herbs
and egg. Season to taste with salt and
pepper and stir well with a wooden spoon
until thoroughly mixed.

❷ Form the mixture into small balls, about
the size of a golf ball, between the palms
of your hands. Spear each one with a
cocktail stick and brush with oil.

❸ Cook over medium-hot coals, turning
frequently and brushing with more oil as
necessary, for 10 minutes, or until cooked
through. Transfer to a large serving plate
and serve immediately with a choice
of sauces.

Variation

Substitute 1 cooked potato and 1 cooked small
beetroot, both finely chopped, for the breadcrumbs.

Bacon Koftas

Koftas – moulded kebabs – are usually made from a spicy mixture of minced lamb.
These ones are economically based on lean bacon. While they are very easy
to make, be careful not to over-process them.

serves 4

1 small onion	1 egg white
225 g/8 oz lean bacon, rinded and roughly chopped	pepper
	paprika, for dusting
85 g/3 oz fresh white breadcrumbs	chopped nuts, for coating (optional)
1 tbsp chopped fresh marjoram	fresh chives lengths, to garnish
grated rind of 1 lemon	bulgar wheat or couscous salad, to serve

Method

❶ Preheat the barbecue. Using a sharp knife, chop the onion, then place it in a food processor with the bacon, breadcrumbs, marjoram, lemon rind and egg white. Season to taste with pepper and process briefly, just until the mixture is blended.

❷ Divide the bacon mixture into 8 equal portions and form each around a skewer into a fat sausage. Dust the skewered koftas with paprika. If you like, form 4 of the portions into rounds rather than sausages, then spread the chopped nuts out on a large, flat plate and roll the rounds in them to coat.

❸ Cook over hot coals for 10 minutes, turning frequently. Transfer to a large serving plate and serve immediately, garnished with fresh chives lengths.

Fabulous Frankfurter Skewers

A new way with an old favourite – cook frankfurter sausages on the barbecue for a wonderful smoky flavour and an incredibly easy meal. They are served here with garlic toast.

serves 4

12 frankfurter sausages

2 courgettes, cut into 1-cm/½-inch slices

2 corn cobs, cut into 1-cm/½-inch slices

12 cherry tomatoes

12 baby onions

2 tbsp olive oil

Garlic toast

2 garlic bulbs

2–3 tbsp olive oil

1 baguette, sliced

salt and pepper

Method

❶ Preheat the barbecue. To make the Garlic Toast, slice off the tops of the garlic bulbs. Brush the bulbs with oil and wrap them in foil. Cook over hot coals, turning occasionally, for 30 minutes.

❷ Meanwhile, cut each frankfurter sausage into 3 pieces. Thread the frankfurter pieces, courgette slices, corn cob slices, tomatoes and onions alternately on to metal skewers. Brush with some of the oil.

❸ Cook the skewers over hot coals, turning and brushing frequently with the oil, for 8–10 minutes. Meanwhile, brush the slices of baguette with the remianing oil and toast both sides on the barbecue. Unwrap the garlic bulbs and squeeze the cloves on to the bread. Season to taste with salt and pepper and drizzle over a little extra oil, if desired. Transfer the skewers to a large serving plate and serve immediately with the Garlic Toast.

Variation

To make Garlic Bread, slice a baguette without cutting it right through. Spread with 2 crushed garlic cloves beaten into 115 g/4 oz butter. Wrap in foil and cook for 15 minutes.

Chicken Tikka

This colourful dish looks immensely appetizing and as it cooks the aroma is out of this world – it lives up to its promise, too.

serves 4

500 g/1 lb 2 oz skinless, boneless chicken, cut into 5-cm/2-inch cubes

1 garlic clove, finely chopped

1-cm/½-inch piece fresh root ginger, finely chopped

150 ml/5 fl oz natural yogurt

4 tbsp lemon juice

1 tsp chilli powder

¼ tsp ground turmeric

1 tbsp chopped fresh coriander

vegetable oil, for brushing

naan bread, to serve

Raita

½ cucumber

1 fresh green chilli, deseeded and finely chopped

300 ml/10 fl oz natural yogurt

¼ tsp ground cumin

salt

To garnish

thinly sliced onion rings

fresh coriander sprigs

lemon wedges

Method

❶ Place the chicken in a large glass bowl. Add the garlic, ginger, yogurt, lemon juice, chilli powder, turmeric and coriander and stir well. Cover with clingfilm and leave to marinate in the refrigerator for up to 8 hours.

❷ Preheat the barbecue. To make the raita, cut the cucumber into thick slices, then chop finely. Place the cucumber and chilli in a bowl and beat in the yogurt with a fork. Stir in the cumin and season to taste with salt. Cover and leave to chill in the refrigerator until required.

❸ Thread the chicken cubes on to presoaked wooden skewers and brush with oil. Cook the chicken over medium-hot coals, turning and brushing frequently with oil, for 15 minutes, or until thoroughly cooked. Briefly heat the naan bread on the barbecue. Remove the chicken from the skewers and place on individual serving plates. Garnish with onion rings, coriander sprigs and lemon wedges and serve with the naan bread and the raita.

Sage & Lemon Poussins

Spatchcocked poussins are the ideal choice for a barbecue, as they
are easy to handle and look attractive. You can buy them ready
prepared or spatchcock them yourself.

serves 4

4 poussins, about 450 g/1 lb each

1 lemon

2 tbsp chopped fresh sage

salt and pepper

To garnish

fresh herb sprigs, such as sage

lemon slices

Method

❶ Preheat the barbecue. To spatchcock the poussins, turn 1 bird breast-side down and, using strong kitchen scissors or poultry shears, cut through the skin and ribcage along both sides of the backbone, from tail to neck. Remove the backbone and turn the bird breast-side up. Press down firmly on the breastbone with the heel of your hand to flatten. Fold the wingtips underneath. Repeat with the remaining poussins.

❷ Thinly slice half the lemon and finely grate the rind of the other half. Mix the lemon rind and sage together in a small bowl. Loosen the skin over the breasts and legs of the poussins and insert the lemon and sage mixture. Tuck in the lemon slices and smooth the skin back firmly. Push a metal skewer into one wing, through the top of the breast and out of the other wing. Push a second skewer into one thigh, through the bottom of the breast and out of the other thigh. Season to taste with salt and pepper.

❸ Cook the poussins over medium-hot coals for 10–15 minutes on each side or until thoroughly cooked. Serve immediately, garnished with fresh herb sprigs and lemon slices.

Hot Red Chicken

Chicken pieces are used in this adaptation of a traditional Indian recipe for spring chickens, but you could substitute spatchcocked poussins if you prefer (see page 128).

serves 4

1 tbsp curry paste

1 tbsp tomato ketchup

1 tsp Indian five-spice powder

1 fresh red chilli, deseeded and finely chopped

1 tsp Worcestershire sauce

1 tsp sugar

salt

8 skinless chicken pieces

vegetable oil, for brushing

To garnish
lemon wedges

fresh coriander sprigs

naan bread, to serve

Method

❶ Place the curry paste, tomato ketchup, five-spice powder, chilli, Worcestershire sauce and sugar in a small bowl, and stir until the sugar has dissolved. Season to taste with salt.

❷ Place the chicken pieces in a large, shallow, non-metallic dish and spoon the spice paste over them, rubbing it in well. Cover with clingfilm and leave to marinate in the refrigerator for up to 8 hours.

❸ Preheat the barbecue. Remove the chicken from the spice paste, discarding any remaining paste, and brush with oil. Cook the chicken over medium-hot coals, turning occasionally, for 25–30 minutes, or until tender and the juices run clear when a skewer is inserted into the thickest part of the meat. Briefly heat the naan bread on the barbecue and serve with the chicken, garnished with lemon wedges and coriander sprigs.

Turkey Rolls

These herb-flavoured rolls conceal a soft centre of melted cheese as a lovely surprise. They are served here with redcurrant relish, but also are delicious with a mild mustard sauce.

serves 4

2 tbsp sunflower oil

salt and pepper

4 tbsp chopped fresh marjoram

4 turkey breast steaks

4 tsp mild mustard

175 g/6 oz Emmenthal cheese, grated

1 leek, thinly sliced

Relish

115 g/4 oz redcurrants

2 tbsp chopped fresh mint

2 tsp clear honey

1 tsp red wine vinegar

Method

❶ Preheat the barbecue. To make the redcurrant relish, place all the ingredients in a bowl and mash well with a fork. Season to taste with salt and pepper. Cover with clingfilm and leave to chill in the refrigerator until required.

❷ Pour the oil into a small bowl, season to taste with pepper and stir in 2 teaspoons of the marjoram. Reserve. Place the turkey steaks between 2 sheets of clingfilm and beat with the side of a olling pin to flatten. Season with salt and pepper and spread the mustard evenly over them. Divide the cheese, leek and remaining marjoram between the turkey steaks, roll up and tie securely with kitchen string.

❸ Brush the turkey rolls with the flavoured oil and cook over medium-hot coals, turning and brushing frequently with the remaining oil, for 30 minutes. Serve immediately with the relish.

Variation

The redcurrant relish can be replaced with cranberry relish, if preferred.

Tarragon Turkey

This economical dish is quick and simple to prepare, and yet tastes absolutely wonderful, not least because poultry and tarragon have a natural affinity.

serves 4

4 turkey breast steaks,
about 175 g/6 oz each
salt and pepper
4 tsp wholegrain mustard

8 fresh tarragon sprigs,
plus extra to garnish
4 smoked back bacon rashers
salad leaves, to serve

Method

❶ Preheat the barbecue. Season the turkey to taste with salt and pepper. Using a round-bladed knife, spread the mustard evenly over the turkey.

❷ Place 2 tarragon sprigs on top of each turkey breast and wrap a bacon rasher around to hold the herbs in place. Secure with a cocktail stick.

❸ Cook the turkey over medium-hot coals for 5–8 minutes on each side. Transfer to serving plates and garnish with tarragon sprigs. Serve with salad leaves.

Fruity Duck

Apricots and onions counteract the richness of the duck. Its high fat content makes it virtually self-basting, so it stays superbly moist. The duck looks particularly elegant garnished with spring onion tassels.

serves 4

4 duck breasts

115 g/4 oz ready-to-eat dried apricots

2 shallots, thinly sliced

2 tbsp clear honey

1 tsp sesame oil

2 tsp Chinese five-spice powder

4 spring onions, to garnish

Method

❶ Preheat the barbecue. Using a sharp knife, cut a long slit in the fleshy side of each duck breast to make a pocket. Divide the apricots and shallots between the pockets and secure with skewers.

❷ Mix the honey and sesame oil together in a small bowl and brush all over the duck. Sprinkle with the five-spice powder. To make the garnish, make a few cuts lengthways down the stem of each spring onion. Place in a bowl of ice-cold water and leave until the tassels open out. Drain well before using.

❸ Cook the duck over medium-hot coals for 6–8 minutes on each side. Remove the skewers, transfer to a large serving plate and garnish with the spring onion tassels. Serve immediately.

Variation

Substitute 4 pork chops for the duck and cook over medium-hot coals for 8–9 minutes on each side, or until thoroughly cooked.

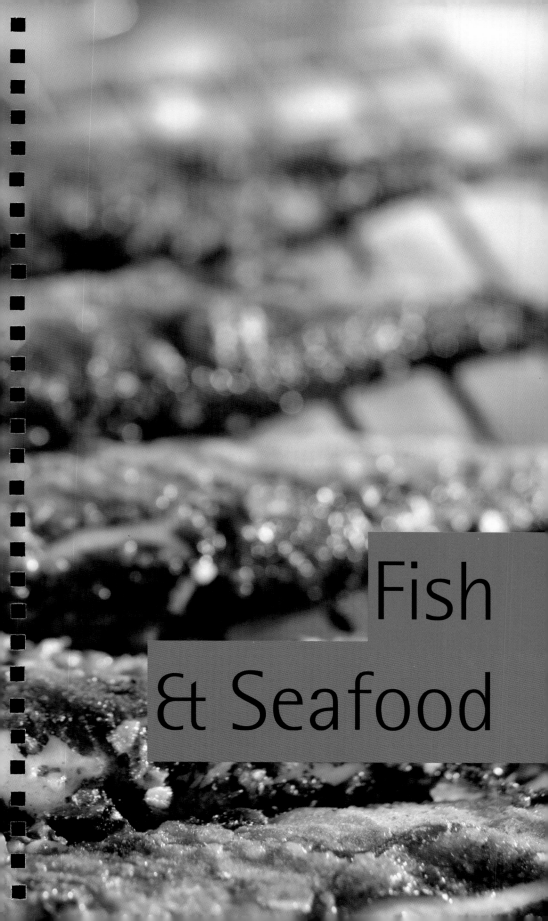

Fish
& Seafood

Caribbean Fish Kebabs

Lightly spiced and marinated, these colourful kebabs look and taste delicious. You can use any firm-textured fish, but for an authentic Caribbean flavour, swordfish is perfect.

serves 6

1 kg/2 lb 4 oz swordfish steaks

3 tbsp olive oil

3 tbsp lime juice

1 garlic clove, finely chopped

1 tsp paprika

salt and pepper

3 onions, cut into wedges

6 tomatoes, cut into wedges

Method

❶ Using a sharp knife, cut the fish into 2.5-cm/1-inch cubes and place in a shallow, non-metallic dish. Place the oil, lime juice, garlic and paprika in a jug and mix well. Season to taste with salt and pepper. Pour the marinade over the fish, turning to coat evenly. Cover with clingfilm and leave to marinate in the refrigerator for 1 hour.

❷ Preheat the barbecue. Thread the fish cubes, onion wedges and tomato wedges alternately on to 6 long, presoaked wooden skewers. Reserve the marinade.

❸ Cook the kebabs over medium-hot coals for 8–10 minutes, turning and brushing frequently with the reserved marinade. When they are cooked through, transfer the kebabs to a large serving plate and serve immediately.

Variation

Instead of serving the kebabs with traditional baked potatoes, serve them with baked sweet potatoes.

140

Salmon with Mango Salsa

Although an oily fish, salmon can dry out easily on the fierce heat of the barbecue. Make sure that it is well coated with the citrus juice before you begin cooking.

serves 4

4 salmon steaks, about 175 g/6 oz each

finely grated rind and juice of 1 lime
or ½ lemon

salt and pepper

Salsa

1 large mango, peeled, stoned and diced

1 red onion, finely chopped

2 passion fruit

2 fresh basil sprigs

2 tbsp lime juice

Method

❶ Preheat the barbecue. Rinse the salmon steaks under cold running water, pat dry with kitchen paper and place in a large, shallow, non-metallic dish. Sprinkle with the lime rind and pour the juice over them. Season to taste with salt and pepper, cover and leave to stand while you make the salsa.

❷ Place the mango flesh in a bowl with the onion. Cut the passion fruit in half. Scoop out the seeds and the pulp with a teaspoon, and add them to the bowl. Tear the basil leaves and add them to the bowl with the lime juice. Season to taste with salt and stir well. Cover with clingfilm and reserve until required.

❸ Cook the salmon steaks over medium-hot coals for 3–4 minutes on each side. Serve immediately with the salsa.

Stuffed Sardines

Barbecued fresh sardines are always a popular choice. They are usually just plainly grilled, but here they are stuffed with herbs and coated in a mild spice mixture.

serves 6

15 g/½ oz fresh parsley, finely chopped

4 garlic cloves, finely chopped

12 fresh sardines, gutted and scaled

3 tbsp lemon juice

85 g/3 oz plain flour

1 tsp ground cumin

salt and pepper

olive oil, for brushing

Method

❶ Place the parsley and garlic in a bowl and mix together. Rinse the fish inside and out under cold running water and pat dry with kitchen paper. Spoon the herb mixture into the fish cavities and pat the remainder all over the outside of the fish. Sprinkle the sardines with lemon juice and transfer to a large, shallow, non-metallic dish. Cover with clingfilm and leave to marinate in the refrigerator for 1 hour.

❷ Preheat the barbecue. Mix the flour and cumin together in a bowl, then season to taste with salt and pepper. Spread out the seasoned flour on a large plate and gently roll the sardines in the flour to coat.

❸ Brush the sardines with oil and cook over medium-hot coals for 3–4 minutes on each side. Serve immediately.

Orange & Lemon Peppered Monkfish

Although monkfish appears quite expensive, there is very little wastage as, apart from the central backbone, the entire tail is edible. Its flavour is meaty and succulent.

serves 6

2 oranges

2 lemons

2 monkfish tails, about 500 g/1 lb 2 oz each, skinned and cut into 4 fillets

6 fresh lemon thyme sprigs

2 tbsp olive oil

salt

2 tbsp green peppercorns, lightly crushed

To garnish

orange wedges

lemon wedges

Method

1 Cut 8 orange slices and 8 lemon slices, reserving the remaining fruit. Rinse the monkfish fillets under cold running water and pat dry with kitchen paper. Place 1 fillet from each monkfish tail, cut-side up, on a work surface and divide the citrus slices between them. Top with the lemon thyme. Reassemble the tails and tie them securely together at intervals with kitchen string or trussing thread. Place the tails in a large, shallow, non-metallic dish.

2 Squeeze the juice from the remaining fruit and mix with the oil in a jug. Season to taste with salt, then spoon the mixture over the fish. Cover with clingfilm and leave to marinate in the refrigerator for up to 1 hour, spooning the marinade over the fish tails once or twice.

3 Preheat the barbecue. Drain the monkfish tails, reserving the marinade. Sprinkle the crushed green peppercorns over the fish, pressing them in with your fingers. Cook the monkfish over medium-hot coals, turning and brushing frequently with the reserved marinade, for 20–25 minutes. Transfer to a chopping board, remove and discard the string and cut the monkfish tails into slices. Serve immediately, garnished with orange and lemon wedges.

Bacon-wrapped Trout

This classic, pan-fried combination is even more delicious cooked on the barbecue, as the smoky flavour of the bacon becomes more pronounced in contrast to the delicate flesh of the fish.

serves 4

4 trout, gutted

4 smoked streaky bacon rashers, rinded

4 tbsp plain flour

salt and pepper

2 tbsp olive oil

2 tbsp lemon juice

lamb's lettuce, to serve

To garnish

fresh parsley sprigs

lemon wedges

Method

❶ Preheat the barbecue. Rinse the trout inside and out under cold running water and pat dry with kitchen paper. Stretch the bacon using the back of a heavy, flat-bladed knife.

❷ Season the flour to taste with salt and pepper and spread it out on a large, flat plate. Gently roll each trout in the seasoned flour until thoroughly coated. Beginning just below the head, wrap a rasher of bacon in a spiral along the length of each fish.

❸ Brush the trout with oil and cook over medium-hot coals for 5–8 minutes on each side or until cooked through and the bacon is crispy. Transfer to 4 large serving plates and drizzle with the lemon juice. Garnish with parsley sprigs and lemon wedges and serve with lamb's lettuce.

Sizzling Scallops

This is a great new way to cook scallops on the barbecue. You can also use other shellfish, such as oysters, if you prefer.

serves 4

rind of 1 lemon

6 tbsp olive oil

salt and pepper

12 prepared scallops

115 g/4 oz fresh wholemeal breadcrumbs

55 g/2 oz butter, melted

lemon wedges, to garnish (optional)

Method

❶ Finely grate the lemon rind, then place it in a dish with the oil and mix together. Season to taste with salt and pepper. Add the scallops, tossing to coat, then cover and leave to marinate for 30 minutes.

❷ Preheat the barbecue. Place the breadcrumbs in a large bowl. Add the scallops, one at a time, and toss until they are well coated, then thread on to individual presoaked wooden skewers. Drizzle with the melted butter.

❸ Cook the breaded scallops over medium-hot coals, turning once, for 8–10 minutes, or until just cooked. Transfer to a large serving dish, garnish with lemon wedges, if desired, and serve immediately.

Chargrilled Devils

This is a barbecue version of the classic appetizer Angels on Horseback (see page 82), and goes to prove how sophisticated and elegant alfresco cooking can be.

serves 4

36 fresh oysters

18 streaky bacon rashers, rinded

1 tbsp mild paprika

1 tsp cayenne pepper

Sauce

1 fresh red chilli, deseeded and finely chopped

1 garlic clove, finely chopped

1 shallot, finely chopped

2 tbsp finely chopped fresh parsley

2 tbsp lemon juice

salt and pepper

Method

❶ Preheat the barbecue. Open the oysters, catching the juice from the shells in a non-metallic bowl. Cut the oysters from the bottom shells, reserve and tip any remaining juice into the bowl. To make the sauce, add the red chilli, garlic, shallot, parsley and lemon juice to the bowl, then season to taste with salt and pepper and mix well. Cover the bowl with clingfilm and leave to chill in the refrigerator until required.

❷ Cut each bacon rasher in half across the centre. Season the oysters with paprika and cayenne, then roll each one up in half a bacon rasher. Spear each wrapped oyster with a presoaked cocktail stick or thread 9 on to each of the 4 presoaked wooden skewers.

❸ Cook over hot coals, turning frequently, for 5 minutes, or until the bacon is well browned and crispy. Transfer to a large serving plate and serve immediately with the sauce.

Variation

You can replace the shallot with a small, finely chopped onion and the fresh parsley with the same amount of snipped fresh chives, if you prefer.

Spanish Prawns

**These fresh prawns are served with a fiery tomato and chilli sauce.
If you prefer a milder flavour, you can reduce the number of chillies.**

serves 6

1 bunch of fresh flat-leaved parsley

36 large, raw Mediterranean prawns,
peeled, with tails left on, and deveined

3–4 tbsp olive oil

lemon wedges, to garnish

Sauce

6 fresh red chillies

1 onion, chopped

2 garlic cloves, chopped

500 g/1 lb 2 oz tomatoes, chopped

3 tbsp olive oil

pinch of sugar

salt and pepper

Method

❶ Preheat the barbecue. Chop enough parsley to fill 2 tablespoons and reserve. To make the sauce, deseed and chop the chillies, then place in a food processor with the onion and garlic and process until finely chopped. Add the tomatoes and oil and process to a purée.

❷ Transfer the mixture to a saucepan set over a very low heat, stir in the sugar and season to taste with salt and pepper. Simmer very gently, without boiling, for 15 minutes. Transfer the sauce to an earthenware bowl and place on the side of the barbecue to keep warm.

❸ Rinse the prawns under cold running water and pat dry on kitchen paper. Mix the reserved parsley and oil together in a dish, add the prawns and toss well to coat. Cook the prawns over medium-hot coals for 3 minutes on each side, or until they have changed colour. Transfer to a plate, garnish with lemon wedges and serve with the sauce.

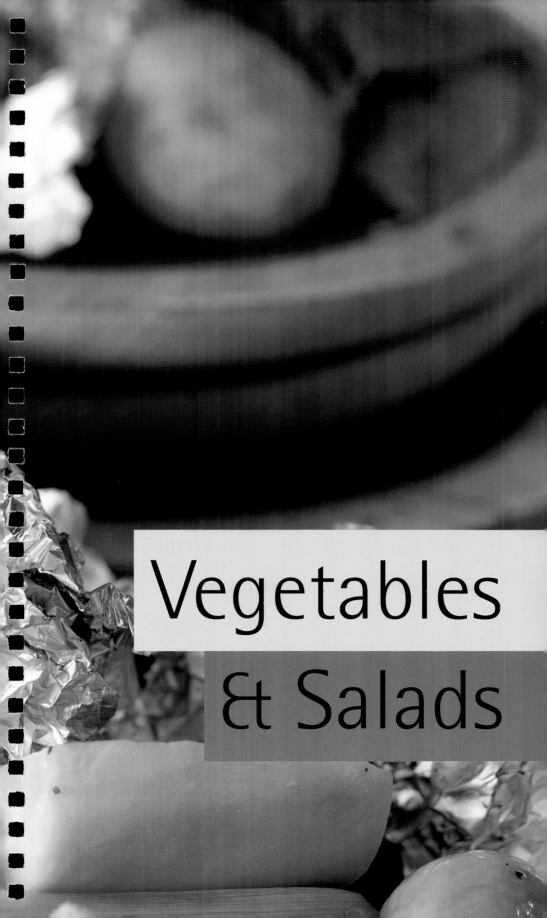

Vegetables
& Salads

Stuffed Tomato Parcels

**An unusual filling for stuffed tomatoes, the spinach and cheese are
given extra flavour with toasted sunflower seeds.**

serves 4

1 tbsp olive oil

2 tbsp sunflower seeds

1 onion, finely chopped

1 garlic clove, finely chopped

500 g/1 lb 2 oz fresh spinach, thick stalks
removed and leaves shredded

pinch of freshly grated nutmeg

salt and pepper

4 beef tomatoes

140 g/5 oz mozzarella cheese, diced

Method

❶ Preheat the barbecue. Heat the oil in a heavy-based saucepan. Add the sunflower seeds and cook, stirring constantly, for 2 minutes, or until golden. Add the onion and cook over a low heat, stirring occasionally, for 5 minutes, or until softened but not browned. Add the garlic and spinach, cover and cook for 2–3 minutes, or until the spinach has wilted. Remove the saucepan from the heat and season to taste with nutmeg, salt and pepper. Leave to cool.

❷ Using a sharp knife, cut off and reserve a thin slice from the top of each tomato and scoop out the flesh with a teaspoon, taking care not to pierce the shell. Chop the flesh and stir it into the spinach mixture with the cheese.

❸ Fill the tomato shells with the spinach and cheese mixture and replace the tops. Cut 4 squares of foil, each large enough to enclose a tomato. Place a tomato in the centre of each square and fold up the sides to enclose securely. Cook over hot coals, turning occasionally, for 10 minutes. Serve immediately in the parcels.

Potato Fans

These garlic-flavoured roast potatoes make a wonderful alternative to baked potatoes. Allow plenty of time for cooking.

serves 6

6 large potatoes, scrubbed but not peeled

2 tbsp garlic-flavoured olive oil

Method

❶ Preheat the barbecue. Using a sharp knife, make a series of cuts across the potatoes almost all the way through. Cut out 6 squares of foil, each large enough to enclose a potato.

❷ Place a potato on each square of foil and brush generously with the garlic-flavoured oil. Fold up the sides of the foil to enclose the potatoes completely.

❸ Cook the foil parcels over hot coals, turning occasionally, for 1 hour. To serve, open the parcels and gently pinch the potatoes to open up the fans.

Courgette & Cheese Parcels

These delicately flavoured, melt-in-the-mouth stuffed courgettes are ideal if you are serving food to both meat-eaters and vegetarians, as the parcels can be cooked in the barbecue embers and so avoid any contact with meat on the grill.

serves 8

8 courgettes

1 tbsp olive oil, plus extra for brushing

115 g/4 oz feta cheese (drained weight),
cut into strips

1 tbsp finely chopped mint

pepper

Method

❶ Preheat the barbecue. Cut out 8 rectangles of foil, each large enough to enclose a courgette, and brush lightly with oil. Cut a slit along the length of each courgette and place them on the foil rectangles.

❷ Insert strips of feta cheese along the slits in the courgettes, then drizzle the oil over the top, sprinkle with the reserved chopped mint and season to taste with pepper. Fold in the sides of the foil and seal the edges securely to enclose the cheese-stuffed courgettes completely.

❸ Bake the courgette parcels in the barbecue embers for 30 minutes. Carefully unwrap the parcels and serve immediately.

Variation

If you prefer, substitute mozzarella cheese or fontina cheese for the feta cheese and replace the mint with the same amount of fresh parsley.

Vegetarian Brochettes

The great thing about tofu – apart from the fact that it is packed with protein – is its ability to absorb other flavours, in this case a mustard and honey flavoured glaze.

serves 4

2 courgettes

1 yellow pepper, deseeded
and quartered

225 g/8 oz firm tofu (drained weight)

4 cherry tomatoes

4 baby onions

8 button mushrooms

Honey glaze

2 tbsp olive oil

1 tbsp Meaux mustard

1 tbsp clear honey

salt and pepper

Method

❶ Preheat the barbecue. Using a vegetable peeler, peel off strips of skin along the length of the courgettes to leave alternate cream and green stripes, then cut each courgette into 8 thick slices. Cut each of the yellow pepper quarters in half. Cut the drained tofu into 2.5-cm/1-inch cubes.

❷ Thread the pieces of pepper, courgette slices, tofu cubes, tomatoes, onions and mushrooms on to 4 metal skewers. To make the glaze, mix the oil, mustard and honey together in a jug and season to taste with salt and pepper.

❸ Brush the brochettes with the honey glaze and cook over medium-hot coals, turning and brushing frequently with the glaze, for 8–10 minutes. Serve.

Variation

You can also make vegetable brochettes. Omit the tofu and use aubergine chunks, courgette chunks and small strips of red pepper.

Summer Vegetable Parcels

You can use any baby vegetables you like – patty pan squash, corn cobs and plum tomatoes look attractive and add colour. Serve with grilled meat or fish for a substantial barbecue main course.

serves 4

1 kg/2 lb 4 oz mixed baby vegetables, such as carrots, patty pan squash, corn cobs, plum tomatoes, leeks, courgettes and onions

1 lemon

115 g/4 oz unsalted butter

3 tbsp chopped mixed fresh herbs, such as parsley, thyme and chervil

2 garlic cloves

salt and pepper

Method

❶ Preheat the barbecue. Cut out 4 x 30-cm/12-inch squares of foil and divide the vegetables equally between them.

❷ Using a grater, finely grate the lemon rind, then squeeze the juice from the lemon and reserve until required. Place the lemon rind, butter, herbs and garlic in a food processor and process until blended, then season to taste with salt and pepper. Alternatively, beat together in a bowl until blended.

❸ Divide the flavoured butter equally between the vegetables, dotting it on top. Fold up the sides of the foil to enclose the vegetables, sealing securely. Cook over medium-hot coals, turning occasionally, for 25–30 minutes. Open the parcels, sprinkle with the reserved lemon juice and serve immediately.

Variation

If baby vegetables are unavailable, then use larger vegetables cut into small pieces, such as courgette and carrot batons and aubergine chunks.

Corn-on-the-Cob with Blue Cheese Dressing

Corn cobs are delicious grilled on the barbecue. Cook them as soon after purchase as possible because they quickly lose their sweetness as their natural sugars convert to starch.

serves 6

140 g/5 oz Danish Blue cheese
140 g/5 oz curd cheese
125 ml/4 fl oz natural Greek yogurt

salt and pepper
6 corn cobs in their husks

Method

❶ Preheat the barbecue. Crumble the Danish Blue cheese, then place in a bowl. Beat with a wooden spoon until creamy. Beat in the curd cheese until thoroughly blended. Gradually beat in the yogurt and season to taste with salt and pepper. Cover with clingfilm and leave to chill in the refrigerator until required.

❷ Fold back the husks on each corn cob and remove the silks. Smooth the husks back into place. Cut out 6 rectangles of foil, each large enough to enclose a corn cob. Wrap the corn cobs in the foil.

❸ Cook the corn cobs over hot coals, turning frequently, for 15–20 minutes. Unwrap the corn cobs and discard the foil. Peel back the husk on one side of each and trim off with a sharp knife or kitchen scissors. Serve immediately with the blue cheese dressing.

Cajun Vegetables

These spicy vegetables would be a perfect accompaniment to some colourful Caribbean Fish Kebabs (see page 140).

serves 4

4 corn cobs
2 sweet potatoes, scrubbed but not peeled
25 g/1 oz butter, melted

Spice mix
2 tsp paprika
1 tsp ground cumin
1 tsp ground coriander
1 tsp pepper
$\frac{1}{2}$–1 tsp chilli powder

Method

❶ Preheat the barbecue. To make the spice mix, mix all the ingredients together in a small bowl.

❷ Remove the husks and silks from the corn cobs, then cut each cob into 4 equal chunks. Cut the sweet potatoes into thick slices, but do not peel. Brush the corn chunks and sweet potato slices with melted butter and sprinkle with some spice mix.

❸ Cook the corn cobs and sweet potatoes over medium-hot coals, turning frequently, for 12–15 minutes. Brush with more melted butter and sprinkle with extra spice mixture during cooking. Transfer the corn and sweet potatoes to a large serving plate and serve immediately.

Prune, Apricot & Onion Skewers

These flavoursome, fruity skewers go well with plain grilled pork chops, duck breasts, lamb steaks or kebabs, as their sweetness counteracts the richness of the meat.

serves 4

500 g/1 lb 2 oz baby onions

175 g/6 oz no-soak prunes, stoned

225 g/8 oz dried apricots, stoned

5-cm/2-inch cinnamon stick

225 ml/8 fl oz white wine

2 tbsp chilli sauce

2 tbsp sunflower oil

Method

❶ Cut the tops off the onions and peel off the skin. Reserve until required. Place the prunes, apricots, cinnamon and wine in a heavy-based saucepan and bring to the boil. Reduce the heat and simmer for 5 minutes. Drain, reserving the cooking liquid, and leave the fruit until cool enough to handle.

❷ Return the cooking liquid and cinnamon stick to the saucepan, return to the boil and boil until reduced by half. Remove the saucepan from the heat and remove and discard the cinnamon stick. Stir in the chilli sauce and oil.

❸ Thread the prunes, apricots and onions on to several metal skewers. Cook over medium-hot coals, turning and brushing frequently with the wine mixture, for 10 minutes. Serve immediately.

Aubergines
with Tzatziki

This makes a delicious appetizer for a barbecue party or can be served as part of a vegetarian barbecue meze with Stuffed Tomato Parcels (see page 158), or Courgette & Cheese Parcels (see page 162).

serves 4

2 tbsp olive oil

salt and pepper

2 aubergines, thinly sliced

Tzatziki

½ cucumber

1 garlic clove

4 spring onions

300 ml/10 fl oz natural Greek yogurt

2½ tbsp chopped fresh mint

salt and pepper

fresh mint sprigs, to garnish

Method

❶ Preheat the barbecue. To make the Tzatziki, follow Steps 1 and 2 on page 16. Transfer to a serving bowl, cover with clingfilm and leave to chill in the refrigerator until required.

❷ Season the oil with salt and pepper, then brush the aubergine slices with the oil.

❸ Cook the aubergines over hot coals for 5 minutes on each side, brushing with more oil, if necessary. Transfer to a large serving plate and serve immediately with the Tzatziki, garnished with mint.

Tropical Rice Salad

Rice salads are always popular and this colourful, fruity mixture goes especially well with barbecued meat or chicken.

serves 4

115 g/4 oz long-grain rice

salt

4 spring onions

225 g/8 oz canned pineapple pieces in natural juice

200 g/7 oz canned sweetcorn, drained

2 red peppers, deseeded and diced

3 tbsp sultanas

Dressing

1 tbsp groundnut oil

1 tbsp hazelnut oil

1 tbsp light soy sauce

1 garlic clove, finely chopped

1 tsp chopped fresh root ginger

salt and pepper

Method

❶ Cook the rice in a large saucepan of lightly salted boiling water for 15 minutes, or until tender. Drain thoroughly and rinse under cold running water. Place the rice in a large serving bowl.

❷ Using a sharp knife, finely chop the spring onions. Drain the pineapple pieces, reserving the juice in a jug. Add the pineapple pieces, sweetcorn, red peppers, chopped spring onions and sultanas to the rice and mix together lightly.

❸ Add all the dressing ingredients to the reserved pineapple juice, whisking well, and season to taste with salt and pepper. Pour the dressing over the salad and toss until the salad is thoroughly coated. Serve immediately.

Variation

Try other flavoured nut oils, such as walnut oil or sesame oil. You can also substitute sunflower oil for the groundnut oil, if you prefer.

Tabbouleh

This Middle Eastern salad is increasingly fashionable. It is a classic accompaniment to lamb, but goes well with most grilled meat.

serves 4

175 g/6 oz bulgar wheat

3 tbsp extra virgin olive oil

4 tbsp lemon juice

salt and pepper

4 spring onions

1 green pepper, deseeded and sliced

4 tomatoes, chopped

2 tbsp chopped fresh parsley

2 tbsp chopped fresh mint

8 black olives, stoned

fresh mint sprigs, to garnish

Method

❶ Place the bulgar wheat in a large bowl and add enough cold water to cover. Leave to stand for 30 minutes, or until the wheat has doubled in size. Drain well and press out as much liquid as possible. Spread out the wheat out on kitchen paper to dry.

❷ Place the wheat in a serving bowl. Mix the oil and lemon juice together in a jug and season to taste with salt and pepper. Pour the lemon mixture over the wheat and leave to marinate for 1 hour.

❸ Using a sharp knife, finely chop the spring onions, then add to the salad with the green pepper, tomatoes, parsley and mint and toss lightly to mix. Top the salad with the olives and garnish with fresh mint sprigs, then serve.

Variation

Use different types of fresh tomatoes – try vine-ripened tomatoes, which have a delicate, sweet flavour, or cherry tomatoes, cut in half.

Cheese & Walnut Pasta Salad

This is an ideal salad to serve with a barbecue, as it is not just a pasta salad, which can seem a little mundane, but also includes a colourful mix of crisp salad leaves.

serves 4

225 g/8 oz dried fusilli
salt and pepper
225 g/8 oz dolcelatte cheese
100 g/3½ oz mixed salad leaves, such
as oak leaf lettuce, radina, baby spinach,
rocket and lamb's lettuce

115 g/4 oz walnut halves
4 tbsp sunflower oil
2 tbsp walnut oil
2 tbsp red wine vinegar

Method

❶ Cook the pasta in a large saucepan of lightly salted boiling water for 8–10 minutes, or until tender, but still firm to the bite. Drain, rinse under cold running water and drain again.

❷ Using a sharp knife, cut the dolcelatte cheese into cubes. Place the salad leaves in a large serving bowl and add the cooked pasta. Sprinkle the cheese on top.

❸ Preheat the grill to medium. Place the walnut halves on a large baking tray and cook under the grill for a few minutes, or until lightly toasted. Leave to cool. Meanwhile, mix the sunflower oil, walnut oil and red wine vinegar together in a jug and season to taste with salt and pepper. Pour the dressing over the salad, toss lightly, then top with the toasted walnuts.

Red & Green Salad

Beetroot and orange is a classic combination and here they are mixed with tender, baby spinach leaves to make a dramatic and colourful warm salad.

serves 4

650 g/1 lb 7 oz cooked beetroot, peeled

3 tbsp extra virgin olive oil

juice of 1 orange

1 tsp caster sugar

1 tsp fennel seeds

salt and pepper

115 g/4 oz fresh baby spinach leaves

Method

❶ Using a sharp knife, dice the cooked beetroot and reserve until required. Heat the oil in a small, heavy-based saucepan. Add the orange juice, sugar and fennel seeds and season to taste with salt and pepper. Stir constantly until the sugar has dissolved.

❷ Add the reserved beetroot to the saucepan and stir gently to coat. Remove the saucepan from the heat.

❸ Arrange the baby spinach leaves and warmed beetroot on a plate and serve immediately. .

Desserts

Mixed Fruit Kebabs

You can use almost any firm-fleshed fruit to make these colourful, quick and easy kebabs. Remember to soak the wooden skewers in cold water before using to prevent burning.

serves 4

2 nectarines, halved and stoned

2 kiwi fruit

4 red plums

1 mango, peeled, halved and stoned

2 bananas, peeled and thickly sliced

8 strawberries, hulled

1 tbsp clear honey

3 tbsp Cointreau

Method

❶ Cut the nectarine halves in half again and place in a large, shallow dish. Peel and quarter the kiwi fruit. Cut the plums in half and remove the stones. Cut the mango flesh into chunks and add to the dish with the kiwi fruit, plums, bananas and strawberries.

❷ Mix the honey and Cointreau together in a jug until well blended. Pour the mixture over the fruit and toss lightly to coat. Cover with clingfilm and leave to marinate in the refrigerator for 1 hour.

❸ Preheat the barbecue. Drain the fruit, reserving the marinade. Thread the fruit on to several presoaked wooden skewers and cook over medium-hot coals, turning and brushing frequently with the reserved marinade, for 5–7 minutes, then serve.

Barbecued Baked Apples

**When they are wrapped in foil, apples bake to perfection
on the barbecue and make a delightful finale to any meal.**

serves 4

4 medium cooking apples	25 g/1 oz stem ginger, chopped
25 g/1 oz walnuts, chopped	1 tbsp Amaretto (optional)
25 g/1 oz ground almonds	50 g/1¾ oz butter
25 g/1 oz light muscovado sugar	whipping cream or natural yogurt,
25 g/1 oz cherries, chopped	to serve

Method

❶ Preheat the barbecue. Core the apples and, using a sharp knife, score each one around the middle to prevent the skins splitting while cooking.

❷ To make the filling, mix the walnuts, almonds, sugar, cherries, ginger and Amaretto, if using, together in a bowl.

❸ Spoon some filling mixture into each apple, pushing it down into the hollowed-out core. Mound a little of the filling mixture on top of each apple.

❹ Place each apple on a large square of double thickness foil and generously dot all over with the butter. Gather up and seal the foil so that the apple is completely enclosed.

❺ Barbecue the foil parcels containing the apples over hot coals for 25–30 minutes, or until tender.

❻ Transfer the apples to warmed, serving plates. Serve with lashings of whipped cream or thick natural yogurt.

Variation

*If the coals are dying down, place the
foil parcels directly on to the coals,
raking them up around the apples.*

Banana Sizzles

**Bananas are particularly sweet and delicious when grilled –
and conveniently come with their own protective wrapping.**

serves 4

3 tbsp butter, softened	pinch of ground cinnamon
2 tbsp dark rum	4 bananas
1 tbsp orange juice	orange zest, to decorate
4 tbsp dark muscovado sugar	

Method

❶ Preheat the barbecue. Beat the butter with the rum, orange juice, sugar and cinnamon in a small bowl until thoroughly blended and smooth.

❷ Place the bananas, without peeling, over hot coals and cook, turning frequently, for 6–8 minutes, or until the skins are blackened.

❸ Transfer the bananas to serving plates, slit the skins and cut partially through the flesh lengthways. Divide the flavoured butter between the bananas, decorate with orange zest and serve.

Recipe List

- Aïoli 14 • Anchovy, Olive & Cheese Triangles 62 • Aubergines with Tzatziki 174
- Baba Ghanoush 26 • Bacon Koftas 122 • Bacon-wrapped Trout 148
- Banana Sizzles 190 • Barbecued Baked Apples 188 • Best Ever Burgers 108
- Böreks 54 • Bruschetta 94 • Cajun Vegetables 170 • Caribbean Crab Cakes 60
- Caribbean Fish Kebabs 140 • Chargrilled Devils 152 • Cheese & Apricot Morsels 58
- Cheese & Bean Pâté 34 • Cheese & Walnut Pasta Salad 180 • Cheese Straws 48
- Chicken Tikka 126 • Corn-on-the-Cob with Blue Cheese Dressing 168
- Courgette & Cheese Parcels 162 • Deep-fried Prawn Balls 64
- Devils & Angels on Horseback 82 • Easy Nibbles 46
- Egg & Tapenade Toasties 42 • Fabulous Frankfurter Skewers 124
- Filled Croustades 44 • Fruity Duck 136 • Guacamole 20
- Honey & Mustard Drumsticks 74 • Hot Red Chicken 130
- Hummus with Lebanese Seed Bread 24 • Indonesian Peanut Fritters 88
- Little Feta & Spinach Crescents 56 • Luxury Cheeseburgers 110
- Meatballs on Sticks 120 • Mini Artichoke Pizzas 92 • Mini Pepperoni Pizzas 90
- Minted Lamb Steaks 114 • Mixed Fruit Kebabs 186
- Moroccan Pickled Vegetables 52 • Mushroom & Chestnut Pâté 32
- Normandy Brochettes 116 • Orange & Lemon Peppered Monkfish 146
- Pigs in Blankets 96 • Potato Fans 160 • Prune, Apricot & Onion Skewers 172
- Quiche Lorraine 50 • Quick Chicken Liver Pâté with Melba Toast 28
- Rack & Ruin 112 • Red & Green Salad 182 • Red Pepper Dip 22
- Sage & Lemon Poussins 128 • Salmon with Mango Salsa 142
- San Francisco Wings 84 • Sausage Rolls 72 • Sausages with Barbecue Sauce 118
- Seafood Filo Parcels 80 • Sicilian Prawns 66 • Sizzling Scallops 150
- Smoked Fish Pâté 30 • Spanish Prawns 154 • Spare Ribs 86
- Spicy Seafood Kebabs 78 • Stuffed Sardines 144 • Stuffed Tomato Parcels 158
- Stuffed Vine Leaves 68 • Summer Vegetable Parcels 166
- Tabasco Steaks with Watercress Butter 106 • Tabbouleh 178 • Taramasalata 18
- Tarragon Turkey 134 • Three-flavour Pinwheels 40
- Traditional English Potted Shrimps 36 • Tropical Rice Salad 176 • Turkey Rolls 132
- Tzatziki 16 • Vegetable Samosas 70 • Vegetarian Brochettes 164